Wolfram Wars

Exposing the Secret
Battle in Portugal

Rod Ashley

An imprint of Bennion Kearny

Published by Dark River, an imprint of Bennion Kearny Limited
6 Woodside
Churnet View Road
Oakamoor
ST10 3AE

Photo and Illustration Credits

About the Author. **Image of author.** Photograph by Moira Ashley.

Introduction. **Figure 1.** Map of Portugal's place in Europe. Source: Wikimedia Commons.

Chapter 1. **Figure 2.** Early maritime discoverers ('Descobrimentos') depicted in the Belem monument on the River Tagus, Lisbon. Source: Wikimedia Commons. | **Figure 3.** Typical Portuguese tiles used for decoration both internally and externally. Source: Author | **Figure 4.** A nineteenth century Portuguese couple dressed in typical rural clothes from Minho Province. Source: Singer sewing machine advertisement card of 1892 on Wiki Commons. | **Figure 5.** Pombaline Lisbon – the modern, post-earthquake, grid-plan of Lisbon (a design adopted by many other cities in years to come). Source: Wikimedia Commons.

Chapter 2. **Figure 6.** Wolfram in its natural state. Source: Wikimedia Commons. | **Figure 7.** Global distribution of wolfram ore. Source: Wikimedia Commons. **Figure 8.** Tungsram. Source: Wikimedia Commons. | **Figure 9.** Tiger Tank abandoned in August 1944 in Vimoutiers, Normandy. It was restored in 1970 as one of only two such models still existing in France. Source: Wikimedia Commons. | **Figure 10.** Estimates created by author from a variety of sources. | **Figure 11.** Worldwide amounts of Tungsten produced by country in 2012. Source: Wikimedia Commons.

Chapter 3. **Figure 12.** University of Coimbra Tower. Photograph by Moira Ashley. | **Figure 13.** Salazar, the young Minister of Finance, reading. Source: Wikimedia Commons. | **Figure 14.** 'Portugal is not a small country' by Henrique Galvão. This propaganda map of 1934 shows Portuguese territories like Angola and Mozambique overlaid over Europe. Source: Cornell University – PJ Mode Collection of Persuasive Cartography.

Chapter 4. **Figure 15.** Palácio Hotel (Courtesy Emma's House in Portugal website). | **Figure 16.** The Duke of Windsor inspecting German troops on his post-abdication visit to Germany; October, 1937. Source: Wikimedia Commons: German Federal Archive. | **Figure 17.** Boeing 314 Yankee Clipper on River Tagus. Source: Wikimedia Commons. | **Figure 18.** Aristedes de Sousa Mendes, Portuguese Consul in Bordeaux, pictured with Rabbi Kruger. Source: Wikimedia Commons. | **Figure 19.** Press cuttings in British Council library, Lisbon relating to Leslie Howard's disappearance. Image by Moira Ashley.

Chapter 5. **Figure 20.** Registration form for Dusko Popov at the Palácio Hotel. Courtesy of Cascais Municipal Historical Archive and Hotel Palácio. | **Figure 21.** The Condes Cinema, frequented by Agent Garbo, taken from the *Suisso Atlántico Hotel.* Image by Moira Ashley. | **Figure 22.** The British Council offices in Lisbon. Image by Moira Ashley.

Chapter 6. **Figure 23.** Registration form for Ian Fleming. Courtesy of Cascais Municipal Historical Archive and Hotel Palácio. |

Chapter 7. **Figure 24.** The Panasqueira mine set high in the Beira Mountains. Image courtesy of Helder Martins Lopes of Pinhal Rural Real Estate. | **Figure 25.** Estimates of Portuguese wolfram (in tons) obtained by Second World War belligerents. British Chamber of

Commerce in Portugal, 1945. | **Figure 26.** Image of derelict Barroca Grande mining village serving Panasqueira mine. Image courtesy of Helder Martins Lopes of Pinhal Rural Real Estate.

Chapter 8. **Figure 27.** Gold stored in the Merkers salt mine, April 1945. Source: The US National Archives and Records Administration (www.archives.gov/research/holocaust/records-and-research/searching-records-relating-to-nazi-gold1.html) | **Figure 28.** Generals Eisenhower and Bradley examining suitcases of gold, gold rings and teeth, December 1945. Source: The US National Archives and Records Administration (www.archives.gov/research/holocaust/records-and-research/searching-records-relating-to-nazi-gold1.html).

Chapter 9. **Figure 29.** Image of deserted Rio de Frades mining village (photo courtesy of Emma Brunton). | **Figure 30.** Image of deserted Rio de Frades mining village (photo courtesy of Emma Brunton) | **Figure 31.** Image of deserted Rio de Frades mining village (photo courtesy of Emma Brunton).

Chapter 10. **Figure 32.** Lisbon's 25 Abril Bridge and the statue of Christ the Redeemer. Source: Wikimedia Commons. | **Figure 33.** Modern apartments in Parque das Nações, Lisbon. Source: Wikipedia Commons.

To my two youngest grandchildren –
Milo Luc Chaillier-Zeiler and Lola Scout Iles.

About the Author

Rod Ashley has a long-standing interest in the Second World War, in economic development and in Portugal, which he has visited on many occasions.

He studied English at the University of Wales and Education at Leicester University, after which he initially pursued a teaching career in both the secondary and further education sectors. In 1991, he was appointed to an academic post in Swansea University's Department of Education and subsequently became an honorary member of the College of Medicine. Having established his own consultancy company, for the last twenty-five years Rod has worked with a diverse range of educational, corporate and European institution clients, as well as formerly being the Director of the Welsh Secondary Schools' Association.

Rod is a Fellow of both the Royal Society of Arts and the Higher Education Academy. He holds the status of Expert Evaluator of researcher career development programmes for the European Commission. A keen motorist, he is the regional Chair of the advanced drivers' organisation, IAM RoadSmart, and is a regular contributor on motoring articles to *Good Motoring* magazine. The author of many books on education, management and career development, Rod is a member of the Historical Association and has, in recent years, completed online American history programmes through the University of Virginia for his own enjoyment.

Married to Moira, Rod lives on the edge of the Gower Peninsula in Swansea, and they enjoy travelling globally in their free time. They have two grown-up daughters and three grandchildren.

Acknowledgements

Writing any book is a partnership effort. Many people have contributed to making this book come to fruition, so the list of those who have assisted is incomplete. However, I would like to thank, in particular, the people mentioned below.

Sofia Leitão of the British Council in Lisbon for her kind welcome and her thorough and exhaustive presentation of archive materials from the war era, particularly those relating to Leslie Howard's lecture tour; Patricia Domingues, PA to the General Manager of the Pálacio Hotel, Estoril, for making time to meet me and for providing the archive materials relating to the guest registration of famous guests; and Rita Prato of Lisbon Walks, for her knowledge of the city of spies. Each of them kindly answered questions before, during and after my research visit.

Professor Margarida Bastos of the Faculty of Sciences at the University of Porto for her kind dedication to tracking down some sources; Professor Otilia Lage of The Faculty of Letters at the University of Porto for permission to quote some of her materials and for answering in depth some follow-up questions.

Helder Lopes of the real estate company www.pinhalrural.com kindly granted permission for images on properties in the Barroca Grande mining village.

Each of these Portuguese nationals displayed the warmth, helpfulness and generosity of their people and made the research artefacts more readily available.

Emma Brunton kindly granted permission for use of photographs of some deserted mining villages. Emma's excellent blog on living in Portugal can be found at: www.emmashouseinportugal.com

My old university friend, John Goldsbrough, formerly of the British Embassy in Lisbon, sparked my initial interest in the subject during our stays with his family in Cascais, and offered advice on arranging my last research visit; Caroline Rauter, Document Services Manager at Swansea University, offered copyright advice; my brother-in-law Kevin McKenna, Group Manager, Systems at GETECH plc provided information on the geological structure of wolfram; and my wife Moira acted as research assistant, providing patient and honest appraisals of draft chapters and valuable suggestions. Any errors and weaknesses remain mine.

My publisher, James Lumsden-Cook of Bennion Kearny provided a thorough review of the manuscript and progressed it efficiently to publication.

My late mother, Irene Ashley, had a love of history and words; my late father, Major Rufus Ashley, made many return visits, post-war, to Bletchley Park. Whilst they never spoke of their wartime experiences, I hope that this book upholds the work of those, like them, who strove for peace.

Rod Ashley, Swansea 2016

Table of Contents

Introduction

How could something as small and flimsy as a light-bulb filament be so crucial to the outcome of the Second World War? Why did neutral Portugal play such a dramatic role in that war? Why was the Lisbon Riviera home to so many double-agents? The answers to these and other questions will soon become clear as we explore a fascinating and little-known sub-plot to a war which has otherwise been written about exhaustively – a shadowy tale of intrigue and double-dealing. It draws in celebrities, secret agents, refugees and royalty, all under the watchful eye of a wily dictator determined to save his own country from warfare.

Wolfram Wars: Exposing The Secret Battle in Portugal focuses on activities in what was largely understood to be an old-fashioned country, quietly getting on with its trade with Great Britain, Brazil and with its colonies in Africa and the Indian Ocean. From 1939 it was neutral, secretive and, as far as many people were concerned, had no important part to play in the global conflict. After all, Portugal was not one of the active, warring partners (known as 'belligerents'), nor was it located in one of the principal theatres of war such as the Far East. Instead, it was a small nation of just over seven-and-a-half million people located on the western fringes of Europe, facing the Atlantic Ocean. Yet Portugal's actions and selective involvement in the war had significant ramifications on both the war's outcome and the relationships between key players. Both Churchill and Roosevelt were closely involved in Portuguese developments throughout the conflict.

In this book, we shall look at the historical factors which placed Portugal in its unique position by virtue of its long-standing relationship with Britain. We'll examine the political, social and economic situation in Portugal in the run-up to the war and discover why its leader, Dr Salazar, decided that the nation should be neutral at the outset and steadfastly remain so throughout the hostilities. Why was he so reluctant to take sides? We'll see what neutrality in warfare actually meant – it did not mean having no involvement at all with belligerent nations. It was in fact a very carefully thought out policy of deliberate actions, albeit at times infuriating for all concerned. We'll find out more about Dr Salazar and why his own brand of politics had an impact not just on Portugal but also on the fortunes of both the Allies and the Nazis.

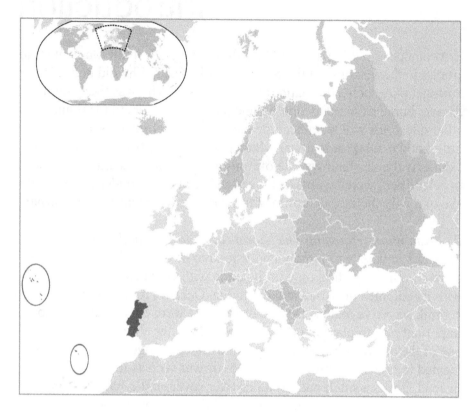

Figure 1. Map of Portugal's place in Europe.

We shall discover what Portugal had to offer both sets of belligerents and why a trading partnership with Salazar's nation was so eagerly sought. At its core, this book is the story of wolfram (also known as tungsten), a key substance used in the manufacture of munitions and in particular to harden machine tools, bullets, shells and tanks.

The main accessible source in Europe of raw wolfram was to be found in rural Portugal and the country was able to maintain its neutrality by skilfully supplying both the Allies and Germany simultaneously. So important was this commodity that espionage became rife, lives were lost and fortunes were made out of arranging its export. We shall also explore what happened to the great wealth that flowed into Portugal as a result of this trade and why, for most of the Portuguese population, this wealth was to have no beneficial impact on the quality of their own lives.

We shall gain an insight into the rapid rise of a new social phenomenon in Portugal, the 'volframistas', those individuals akin to the gold-diggers and entrepreneurs of the nineteenth century American Wild West, who were driven by the mining fever to secure personal wealth. Their extensive impact upon the local economy of the mining areas was matched only by the accompanying social disintegration which remained long after the demand for wolfram dried up.

We shall learn how, at the same time that this lucrative trade was taking place to the benefit of a small number of people, Portugal was offering refuge to those fleeing from elsewhere in mainland Europe. These incoming refugees included many Jews and social groups who were at risk from the Nazis. Fearing for their lives, they existed in desperate conditions whilst awaiting their exit papers. Whether their departures would be aboard crowded transatlantic ships or, for wealthier refugees, on a flight out, their escape remained a dangerous prospect, risking possible arrest, interrogation by the secret police or deportation. Remaining in Lisbon might mean living in destitution, physical and emotional hardship and the risk of being separated from family members who did escape successfully. Intriguingly, the list of refugees also included banished members of several European royal families, basking in the comparative luxury and peace of the Lisbon Riviera. Somehow, these two very different social groups were to co-exist in a small area of Portugal around Lisbon.

Infiltrating all this human and freight traffic, the Portuguese secret police and secret agents from both Britain and Germany kept a watchful eye on everyone. Many of these agents were shadowy and anonymous figures. Others were much more high-profile, with job titles which sounded innocent enough. They included one British 'government official' by the name of Ian Fleming who was later to use his wartime Portuguese experiences to bring to life his fictional creation, James Bond.

Collectively, these activities represent a story well worth telling – of how, for a few years, wartime Portugal was a place of intrigue and influence and how, towards the end of the war, it unravelled into an impoverished dictatorship which was to remain secretive and oppressed for another thirty years until the Carnation Revolution of 1974. But let's start at the beginning and consider what gave rise to this complex situation.

Chapter 1
The Old Portugal

You don't need to have travelled to Portugal to know what some of its principal industries are, nor the strength of the nation's links with Britain. If you think of traditional Portuguese products, those most likely to come to mind are port, wine, cork, sardines and hand-embroidered articles, all of them well-established industries over many centuries. So how did these industries develop and how are they so closely associated with Britain?

In fact, Portugal's association with Britain stretches right back to 1147 when English Crusaders aided the Portuguese in the Conquest of Lisbon from the Moors. The relationship was sealed by the 1373 Anglo-Portuguese Alliance, signed in St Paul's Cathedral in London by King Edward III and the envoys of the Portuguese monarch, Dom Fernando. The Treaty remains the oldest, still active strategic alliance in the world and it has brought mutual benefits over the centuries, starting with the despatch of English archers to ward off the attacks from Castile in 1385. An enduring relationship was formalised when, in 1386, John of Gaunt, the son of King Edward III, agreed that his daughter Philippa would marry Dom Joao I of Portugal. The latter became father to a whole generation of princes who led Portugal into the golden Age of Discoveries.

In 1580, however, Spain invaded Portugal and forced a union which lasted for sixty years until 1642, when a fresh treaty was signed with Britain, cemented by the marriage of Catherine of Braganza to King Charles II of England. The Spanish were defeated by joint Portuguese and British forces and the new treaty guaranteed future Portuguese independence from Spain. The relationship between Britain and Portugal remained strong over the following centuries and was to prove vital in the Second World War in helping secure an Allied victory.

The birth of a maritime explorer nation

It was in the 15th and 16th centuries that Portugal first became a powerful maritime nation. Its many discoverers ('Descobrimentos') set off on perilous journeys into the unknown, finding new continents and nations. These discoverers, with the royal backing of Prince Henry 'the Navigator' in particular, included Bartolomeu Dias who rounded the Cape of Good Hope and entered the Indian Ocean in 1488, and Vasco de Gama who created a maritime route from Portugal to India a decade later. The first circumnavigation of the globe was undertaken by Magellan between 1519 and 1522, an act of unheard of bravery which literally changed mankind's perspective of the world. The discoverers' great achievements are celebrated today in the imposing monument on the north bank of the River Tagus in Belem, just downriver from central Lisbon. Returning from their travels, the discoverers brought wealth, knowledge, experience and a vision which enabled Portugal to develop its own far-flung empire. Angola and Mozambique in east Africa, the island of Goa off the coast of India, Macao and Timor in the Far East and, of course, Brazil, became its greatest colonial assets and they still retain considerable cultural and trading links with Portugal today. Some historians[1] trace the founding of the slave trade to Portugal's export of Africans in the 14th century from the east coast and across the Atlantic.

Figure 2. Early maritime discoverers ('Descobrimentos') depicted in the Belem monument on the River Tagus, Lisbon.

Traditional industries in the old Portugal

For centuries, Portugal was dominated by its traditional industries, principally maritime and agricultural. Maritime industries relied on natural resources: the abundant fish stocks, a topography which

---

[1] Bhasker M. http://www.globalresearch.ca/the-real-first-world-war/5395497.

allowed for the development of both small fishing ports and large international ports, including the river port of Lisbon; and a climate which supported a range of grape varieties, as well as the raising of cattle for both food and leather. All these industries could be carried on in traditional, time-honoured ways without post-industrial revolution machinery, techniques or high-level skills and training. It was essentially a subsistence economy, albeit with specialist input in particular areas.

Port wine

Many port bottlers have British names – alphabetically they include Cockburn, Croft, Dow, Graham's, Sandeman, Taylor Fladgate and Warre. The names alone attest to the breadth of the business, centred on coastal Oporto, and to long-standing Anglo-Portuguese heritage and links over many centuries. In Shakespeare's *King Henry IV, Part 1*, the lovable rogue Sir John Falstaff is accused of selling his soul to the devil *"on Good Friday last for a cup of Madeira and a cold capon's leg."*[2] Madeira wine has been created and bottled on the eponymous Portuguese island for centuries by, amongst others, the old British family Blandy, who continue to market it in a range of suitably British aristocratically-named varieties. As with port wine, the expertise of the British lay in knowing what the market demanded and in creating blends to suit the export palates and, through their commercial success, they established considerable long-standing influence in the wine region of the Douro Valley, in the city of Porto and on the island of Madeira.

Cork

Even today, Portugal is the world's principal grower and exporter of cork[3], harvested from the cork oak tree which dominates the nation's inland landscape. Cork is used not just in the drinks industry but for a variety of purposes in decoration, buoyancy and insulation. Still vital to

---

[2] Shakespeare W. (c.1597). *King Henry IV, Part 1*. Act 1, Scene iii.

[3] Production accounts for 33% of global output. Source: Cork Quality Council, 2004.

the national economy, you will never find a synthetic cork in Portuguese wine bottles!

For centuries, Portugal has been famed for its ceramics, particularly small decorative tiles. Frequently blue (and known as 'azulejos'), these are often arranged pictorially to create murals or to decorate the outside of houses or municipal buildings.

Figure 3. Typical Portuguese tiles used
for decoration both internally and externally.

Fish and leather

All around the coast, both the picturesque and the industrial harbours emit the aroma of sardines, whether they be freshly-caught, smoked, grilled or canned. Sardines are exported around the world and have been for centuries. Additionally, high-quality leather work abounds in Portugal, principally footwear, saddlery, belts and bags. Not usually produced in large-scale factories, these items were historically delivered in part-made format to rural artisans who, paid by piece-work, would complete the items at home, ready for collection by pack-donkey the following week. Frequently, this work would fit in around other subsistence farming tasks to help make ends meet.

Figure 4. A nineteenth century Portuguese couple dressed in typical rural clothes from Minho Province.

18th Century Attempts at Modernisation

Attempts to modernise Portugal were undertaken in the 1700s by the Marques de Pombal, Secretary of State to Dom Jose 1, a monarch who found hunting and opera more enticing pursuits than ruling his country, and who passed significant responsibilities of government to his minister. Heavily-influenced by the Age of Enlightenment across Protestant Europe, Pombal attempted to instil a more open, rational society, whose underpinning philosophy was encapsulated in his

Chapter 1

response to the huge earthquake in Lisbon of 1755: "Bury the dead, heal the living". Pombal's modern mind-set is exemplified by his 1761 decree which ensured that skin colour was no bar to Portuguese citizenship and which made the use of derogatory names for those from the colonies a statutory offence. He created a forerunner of the European concept of 'protected designation of origin' (PDO) in the form of the Douro Wine Company, thus ensuring the quality of port wine. He also introduced Mathematics and Natural Science in the revered University of Coimbra, streamlined the administration of colonial Brazil, and expelled Jesuits for what he considered their disproportionate influence on society.

However, many historians consider his tactics to have been authoritarian and heavy-handed, setting the tone for future autocracy. Whilst his far-reaching social reforms were not fully embraced, his enduring legacy is the 'Pombaline Lisbon' – the open squares, the low-rise, earthquake-proof buildings, the spaciousness and grace which still make the heart of Lisbon one of Europe's most elegant capitals. Even today, a view from the top of Parque Eduardo VII confirms his inspired vision for the city.

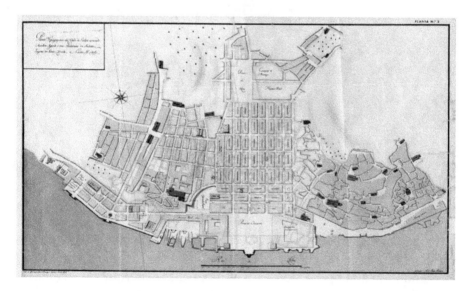

Figure 5. Pombaline Lisbon – the modern, post-earthquake, grid-plan of Lisbon (a design adopted by many other cities in years to come).

So, by the early twentieth century, Portugal was a nation punching above its weight in international trade and discovery, but one which was hampered by its traditional economy. Attempts to modernise it had not lasted and in many ways the industrial revolution in other parts of Europe had passed it by.

The First Republic, 1910-1926

Politically, the early part of the twentieth century saw unrest in Portugal, as elsewhere in Europe. Overthrowing its constitutional monarchy in 1910, a republic was established. Within a month of the revolution, the British government had recognised the new republic, expressing that it was "the liveliest wish of His Britannic Majesty to maintain friendly relations" with Portugal. Centuries of monarchy had seen the expansion of Portugal into a significant global power discovering new countries, continents and maritime routes, so what did the new republic stand for?

Lloyd-Jones[4] argues that throughout its entire sixteen year history from 1910-1926, the First Republic struggled to legitimise itself. Its positive principles are more difficult to detect than what it stood *against* – one of its key tenets was anti-clericalism, since the republic associated the Roman Catholic Church with the Monarchy, and disliked intensely its associated power and pomp. Separation of Church and State was crucial in the government's eyes (enshrined in a new law in 1911), and it also closed convents and seminaries. In particular, it disliked religious orders and expelled some from the country; marriage was deemed purely a civil contract and divorce was permitted. Not surprisingly, there would be a backlash from this approach, particularly from the nation's future leader, Dr Salazar, who had been immersed in the Church throughout his early life.

Against such a tumultuous background, when the First World War broke out in 1914, Portugal was neutral and remained so for two years, despite the threat of German annexation to its colonies of Angola and Mozambique. From being a neutral provider of supplies to the Allies

---

[4] Lloyd-Jones S. *A Short History of the First Republic*. Instituto Universitário de Lisboa, Lisboa, Portugal. 17 March 2000. (Working Paper).

Chapter 1

(principally of food and leather goods), its role changed in 1916 when a German attack brought the nation into the war on the side of the Allies. For Portugal, the impact of the war was both financial and social.[5] It was estimated to have cost nearly one-and-a-half million escudos, over 8,000 lives, nearly 14,000 injured combatants and it deepened the economic recession from which the government was trying to extricate itself.[6]

Austerity measures were unpopular and their impact was to bring about the demise of the First Republic. Cumulatively, these factors brought about a distaste for future engagement in war, a view shared passionately by the new national leader, Dr Antonio de Oliveira Salazar.

---

[5] http://www.portugal1914.org/portal/en/history/the-1914-1918-war/item/6549-economic-impact-of-the-great-war-in-portugal

[6] Intriguingly, in the New Forest, Hampshire, UK, are the remains of a First World War Portuguese army camp. The plaque reads: *"This is the site of a hutted camp occupied by a Portuguese army unit during the First World War. This unit assisted the depleted local labour force in producing timber for the war effort. The Forestry Commission have retained the fireplace from the cookhouse as a memorial to the men who lived and worked here and acknowledge the financial assistance of the Portuguese government in its renovation."* In fact, the Portuguese workers were later replaced in timber production duties by Canadians and Finns who were considered more adept at the work because they provided their own more modern equipment. This is symptomatic of the problem faced in the early twentieth century by traditional Portuguese industry. But it also begs the question: why Britain did not supply the equipment?

Chapter 2
The Magic of Wolfram

How did chemical element $(FeMn)WO_4$, found underground in a number of countries around the world, become so important for 20th century life and play such a pivotal role in the Second World War?

What is wolfram?

Wolfram is a shiny, highly sought-after ore. The refined product is widely referred to as tungsten. Its name is derived from the Swedish words 'tung sten' meaning 'heavy stone'. After mining the tungsten is separated from the chemical compounds, yielding a mined concentration of 76.5% WO_3 (wolframite), of which the usable and tradeable concentrate is around 65% WO_3.[1] This is a high concentration for a mineral and thus makes it cost-effective to transport for refining.

Figure 6. Wolfram in its natural state.

---

[1] Meinert L. (2013). *Tungsten deposits in the Context of Critical Minerals and World Supplies*. US Geological Survey. From presentation given at GEUS Tungsten Assessment Workshop. Available at: http://tinyurl.com/zwgqja4

Chapter 2

Discovered by the Swedish chemist Carl Scheele (hence the name Scheelite, the term for tungsten in some countries), a complex interplay has arisen between the terms tungsten, scheelite, wolfram, and wolframite. This book will refer to the product predominantly as 'wolfram'.

Properties of refined wolfram (tungsten)

Tungsten and its alloys are amongst the hardest of all metals. Tungsten itself has the highest melting point of all pure metals (3,422 degrees Centigrade), which is one thousand degrees above most metals and 800 degrees above its rival, molybdenum. It is also resistant both to oxidisation and to acid attack. This makes it ideal for a number of industrial and commercial applications, where it is used, for example, in electrical contacts, arc-welding electrodes, LCD units and X-ray tubes.

However, tungsten's unique benefit is in conditions which generate enormous heat. If you have used a power-drill you will have seen (and smelt) how the drill-bit reacts as it penetrates certain materials. Drilling into a wall may provide different stages of resistance and rates of progress as you encounter different materials – quick though plaster then slower through brick or concrete block, whilst drilling through wood can create a smoke plume. Cheap drill-bits will buckle – you need tungsten-tipped ones. Likewise, tungsten can be used in the steel-making process to strengthen steel. These days tungsten carbide (sometimes called 'coated cemented carbide') is used in 80-90% of all cutting tool inserts because of its unique combination of toughness and wear resistance and, importantly, its ability to be formed in complex shapes.

In times of war, these resistant qualities are paramount and give enormous strategic advantage. Using tungsten not only reinforces armaments to resist penetration by enemy bullets and shells, but it also means that you can harden the tips of your own armaments so that they can penetrate the enemy's inferior defence equipment. Tungsten's resistance to high temperatures and its strength in alloys has made it a vital raw material for the armaments industry, used for armour-piercing shells and the production of high-speed cutting tools for manufacturing a great variety of armaments.

Wolfram: a sought-after commodity

To keep pace with the demand of the industrial needs of northern Europe in the nineteenth and twentieth centuries, supplies had to be quickly found beyond the mining reserves in Spain, Portugal and Russia. As the United States experienced its own industrial revolution and created the world's largest automotive industry, supplies of wolfram from Canada and South America for developing machine tools were fully-utilised for this market and not exported. The map below indicates the global distribution of wolfram ore.

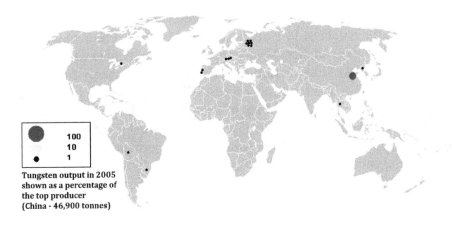

Figure 7. Global distribution of wolfram ore.

With the emergence of Nazi rule in the 1930s, Germany's own automotive and other industries responded to the political call for re-armament. However, the Depression of the late 1920s through to the mid-1930s, affecting the whole of Europe and North America, had impacted upon trading relations between Germany and China, despite the signing of a Sino-German cooperation. During the four-year period from 1937 to 1941, Germany made two fatal errors concerning its supply of wolfram.

Firstly, the outbreak of the Second Sino-Japanese War in July 1937 destroyed much of the progress and promises made in nearly a decade of intense Sino-German cooperation. Under such cooperation, China supplied Germany with tungsten and, in return, bought German machines and weaponry. However, Germany identified that Japan had greater military power to resist Communism, so it was Hitler's foreign policy that would prove the most detrimental factor in Sino-German relations – he chose Japan rather than China as his ally against the Soviet Union.

Secondly, once the Second World War was underway, Germany committed itself in the late summer of 1941 to an advance upon Moscow, even though it would coincide with the notoriously harsh weather conditions of the onset of the bleak Russian winter. Indeed, the period 1941-1944 is crucial in the story of wolfram mining which we'll see unfold, at a time when Portugal was one of the leading global suppliers. (Ironically for Hitler, the largest wolfram deposits within Europe were to be discovered on his own doorstep in Mittersill, Austria in 1967.) Many military analysts have viewed the Moscow winter campaign as the height of folly, pandering only to the Führer's ego, and losing many German soldiers who were then no longer able to fight on other war-fronts. As Giles Milton records[2], in a single twenty-four hour period in December 1941 a staggering 14,000 German soldiers had frost-bitten limbs amputated. Many of these poorly-dressed combatants would be dead within a few days. It was not only limbs and lives which were lost in such a foolhardy campaign – Hitler permanently lost his access to the enormous Soviet wolfram mines. So, in a matter of several years, Germany had lost its two prime suppliers of an increasingly precious commodity.

Spain, like Portugal, would hold a neutral status in the Second World War. Spanish wolfram was available in German-owned mines in the Galicia region but, of course, the country was economically shattered by its own Civil War in the 1930s. Furthermore, given the previous Nazi support for Spain's leader, General Franco, Germany paid for supplies of wolfram in the form of reducing Spanish debt repayments rather than in any hard currency.

Further afield, Australia was also a source of wolfram, but simply too far away for its reliable transportation and, in any case, it was part of the British Empire. So this left Portugal as by far the largest supplier of wolfram for Germany's precision engineering demands and manufacture of its armaments.

---

[2] Milton G. 2011. *Wolfram: The Boy Who Went to War*. London. Sceptre.

After being promoted as Germany's Minister of Armaments and War Production in 1943, Albert Speer actually drove all the way from the German capital – right across Nazi-occupied France and General Franco's neutral Spain – to meet the Portuguese leader, Dr Salazar. Speer was formerly the architect of Nazi Berlin, and he knew the Prime Minister from previous negotiations about supplying marble from the Portuguese African territory of Angola for the edifices which were the visual symbol and reinforcement of the Nazi dream. Speer's mission this time was different – Germany desperately needed wolfram for its planned V2 rockets with which Hitler was planning to attack London. If the nozzles of the rocket jets were constructed of any material inferior to wolfram they would disintegrate on take-off and the entire plan would be a failure. Only wolfram's hardness, elasticity and ability to withstand high-temperature would suffice.

Wolfram and radio communication

Some readers will recall vividly the name Tungsram, a Hungarian manufacturer of light-bulbs, radio and TV valves available widely in Britain for decades. Now part of the giant US General Electric group, Tungsram's name was created in 1896 as a combination of 'tungsten' and 'wolfram'. The company was awarded a patent for electric bulbs with a tungsten filament in 1903.

Figure 8. Tungsram.

Tungsram was also a manufacturer of radio valves, a key component for wartime radio operators, whether in the field or on espionage duty. Despite carrying spares, the prospect of blown valves was a constant source of fear to radio operators on both sides. After the Normandy invasions, the Americans targeted battlefield communications in order to spread confusion among the German troops so that their commanders did not know which forces were attacking and which were retreating. It took an average of only two hours for the Americans to locate the position of the enemy's field radios.

Chapter 2

Wolfram and armaments

As we have mentioned earlier, wolfram is used not just to harden metals themselves but also in machine-tools to cut softer metals. Any manufacturing process for tools is likely to use a tungsten carbide cutting, grinding or chamfering tool to get the smooth and accurate finish required. And this process itself would include the precise machining of most types of weapons and ammunition, from bullets to shells to grenades, as well as larger-scale armaments, such as tanks.

Two tanks are forever associated with the Second World War, the German Panzer and the American Sherman M4. The Sherman was the lighter and more versatile of the two, more manoeuvrable, and well-suited to agile work. Its 75mm shells with a 60-metre range meant that it had to be close to its target to be effective however.

By contrast, the Panzer, with its 88m anti-aircraft weapon shoe-horned into the structure, had an enormous 1600 metre range. With frontal armour up to 4" thick, it seemed impervious to anything the Allies could throw at it, and was known as a 'mobile pill-box'. Introduced in April 1942 on Hitler's birthday, at 56 tons it was the heaviest and largest tank ever built – not surprisingly, it was also unwieldy and inflexible. The Führer's obsession with creating larger, heavier and more cumbersome tanks was an example of the limitations of his strategic thinking. The Germans continually developed their Panzer models throughout the war and by the time of the Normandy landings, the virtually-unassailable Panzer Tiger was a key obstacle for the Allied forces. In the unattributed words of one commander, the Sherman was no contest for the Panzer Tiger:

> *"In order to take out a Tiger, I needed to hit its flanks from 60 yards, whereas it could take me out at 200 yards straight on."*[3]

Such fearsome characteristics induced in Allied soldiers what was known as 'Tiger Terror'. As Dougherty[4] outlines, during the Allies'

---

[3] Quoted in Christopher J. (2014). *Sherman M4 Tank*. Stroud: Amberley Publishing.

invasion, there were fewer than one hundred Tigers in Normandy but their firepower was phenomenal – in one action, five Panzer Tiger I's were able to destroy thirty Allied armoured vehicles with no loss themselves. Its development and deployment used huge amounts of wolfram, even when supplies were dwindling in the last year of the war and it was necessary to fit smaller gun turrets.

Figure 9. Tiger Tank abandoned in August 1944
in Vimoutiers, Normandy. It was restored in 1970 as
one of only two such models still existing in France.

In the Nazis' last-gasp Battle of the Bulge in the Belgian Ardennes (December 1944 - January 1945), the Tiger II was a formidable foe, almost impregnable, virtually unassailable from the front with its enhanced protection, but vulnerable from the flanks if only the Allies could attack it side-on. On a number of occasions, this happened. One American soldier recalls seeing, from a hidden position, a convoy of Tigers passing along a road, allowing the Allies a rare opportunity to

---

[4] Dougherty M J. (2010). *Tanks from World War 1 to the Present Day.* London: Amber Books. p157

fire at the flanks, thus destroying them. Allied crews relied on destroying a Tiger before it could aim its painfully slow-turning gun turret onto them. Given that the weaponry of the Tiger II could penetrate over five inches[5] of Allied armour, it was these lucky escapes which contributed to the Allied victory in the Ardennes.

Wolfram mining today

Mining exploration continually reveals new deposits with supply and demand affecting the global price of all raw materials. There is even a new wolfram mine being developed in Devon[6], UK. Today China currently produces over 87% of total world tungsten production, dwarfing all other sources and stifling competition, whilst Portugal accounts now for only around 1% of global production as there is little scope for expansion in production.

Country / Continent	Production in Tons	% of Global Production (2010)
China	67,000	87%
Russia	2,800	3.6%
Bolivia	1,200	1.6%
Vietnam	1,150	1.5%
Austria	1,000	1.3%
Portugal	**800**	**1.0%**
Africa	800	1.0%
Peru	550	0.7%
Canada	400	0.5%
Thailand	250	0.3%
Brazil	250	0.3%
Spain	250	0.3%
Mongolia	200	0.3%
Other	200	0.3%
Total	**76,850**	**100%**

Figure 10. Wolfram production estimates created by author from a variety of sources.

[5] Fortey G & Livesey J. (2012). *The Complete Guide to Tanks and Armoured Fighting Vehicles*. Wigston, Leicestershire: Southwater.

[6] Wilson J. Tungsten miner hardens big plans in Devon. *Financial Times*, 27 January 2014.

The map below shows recent worldwide production estimates (2012) and highlights China's dominance over the global supply.

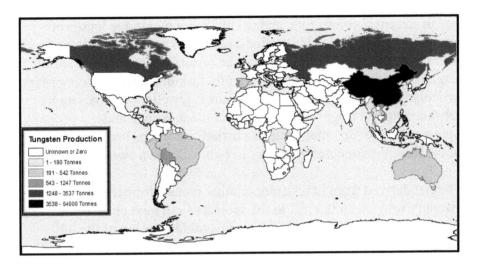

Figure 11. Worldwide amounts of Tungsten produced by country in 2012.

In contrast to the Second World War when the Allies and Axis powers were the dominant consumers, China is currently both the largest producer and consumer of tungsten, accounting for 50% of world demand. This is because it produces many of the electronics and mobile telephony products which are tungsten-hungry. If, for any reason, China were to cease using tungsten and other valuable metals in electronic devices of all sorts, there would be a catastrophic shortage of such equipment and prices would skyrocket.

Modern uses of wolfram

The tungsten derived from wolfram is considered to be one of the world's most precious resources, given its dwindling and finite supply. So much so that in 2012 Berkshire Hathaway, the investment company run by the world's most successful investor, Warren Buffett, bought 25% of the largest wolfram mine outside of China.

Wolfram has many non-military uses, too. Today, about half of it is used as tungsten carbide in drill-bits and other cutting tools. The refined product has a variety of everyday uses – as the filament in a

Chapter 2

traditional light-bulb, as a sharp tip or cutting edge in products like roller blades, hiking poles, razors and in many electronic devices. Most of us use tungsten in some form every day without realising it. It is used in electrical connectors, and (in tiny amounts) in the lenses of sunglasses or in tinted vehicle windscreens. Given all the virtues of wolfram as a 'strategic mineral' and the resultant tungsten as a hard metal, it is perhaps odd that it is currently fashionable as wedding rings, particularly for men. As one UK high-street jeweller promotes on its website, tungsten rings 'are the height of modern style and sophistication for any man getting married' – perhaps less attractive should they require careful surgery to remove from a swollen finger!

Whether derived from tungsten or another metal, 'fripperies' such as jewellery were of no interest to the subject of our next chapter, the autocratic dictator of Portugal during this middle period of the 20th century, Dr Antonio de Oliveira Salazar.

Chapter 3
Salazar the Dictator

Portugal's story during these years is also the story of its leader, Dr Antonio de Oliveira Salazar. How could one man wield so much influence and what factors shaped his character, ideals and, ultimately, his actions? This chapter will analyse the rise of Salazar the statesman and reveal a little more about Salazar the man. We shall learn how Salazar's deeply-held beliefs, developed in his formative years, together with his uncompromising personality, made a significant contribution to the conduct and outcome of the Second World War.

The making of a future dictator

Antonio de Oliveira Salazar was born in 1889 in the central Portuguese region of Beira Alta (which would prove to be one of the regions affected deeply by wartime wolfram mining). As sometimes happened in Portuguese families, he took his mother's surname, Salazar, rather than his father's. She was the more influential parent, who set her own and her son's ambitions above those achieved by her husband. Whilst not wealthy, his parents were landowners in what was essentially a feudal system and they could afford for him to attend school. Like many other intelligent boys of his generation, he was guided into a Roman Catholic seminary between the ages of 11 and 18 with the prospect of training to become a priest. This early childhood shaped an acceptance of authority in him, as well as obedience and, a concept which is difficult for a modern, secular society to comprehend, that of the 'grace of suffering'. However, whilst he remained devout throughout his life, another calling beckoned.

Salazar studied law and economics at the venerable University of Coimbra, renowned for both its intellectual rigour and its traditional values. He then embarked on post-graduate studies, taking his doctorate in 1918 after he had already begun teaching economics there. Whilst at Coimbra, he also led a group of Roman Catholic intellectuals – the Academic Centre for Christian Democracy (or CADC) – who criticised the First Republic for its economic and social instability, as well as its anti-clerical stance. Through this involvement, Salazar started to establish himself as an influential economist.

Figure 12. University of Coimbra Tower.

In 1921, Salazar was elected to the National Assembly as a representative of the CADC, although it was, for him, an unhappy experience.[1] His political career took off from 1926 when the military powers overthrew the First Republic. After a mere five days, his strict austerity proposals had been thrown out by the military government. Just two years later, however, he was being regarded as the potential saviour of the Portuguese economy and nation, and by July 1932 he was appointed Premier – a post he would hold until incapacitated by a brain haemorrhage in September 1968.

---

[1] Wilsford D (ed). 1995. *Political Leaders of Contemporary Western Europe: A Biographical Dictionary.* Westport, Connecticut: Greenwood Press.

Father of the nation

A love affair which turned sour at an early age is the only romantic association Salazar had. There was, though, one woman who remained loyal: his housekeeper Maria, who had first served him in 1915 when he was a student, remained with him throughout his life, introducing into the household two little girls, one an orphan. He treated them both as surrogate daughters, expressing regret that he never had a marriage or children of his own. However, Salazar was wedded to another concept – fatherhood of the nation.

Once elected as Prime Minister, he embraced the concept of 'primus inter pares' ('first among equals'), filling his Cabinet with fellow academics, though none as intellectually capable as himself. He showed total dedication to his political cause and expected the same of others. Indeed, he was fearful of a future Portugal which did not embrace the same principles that he espoused. These principles were to make his handling of both the wolfram and the Azores issues particularly tricky for others to deal with, as we shall see, to the extent that on more than one occasion, Churchill described him as 'impossible'. Financial and organisational skills such as his were in short supply at the time and, perhaps because of a lack of trust in others, between 1932 and 1939 he held multiple Cabinet portfolios. He loved the detail of policies, rigorously interrogating their political, financial and theoretical bases as if he were reading a doctoral thesis. Similarly, he brought an intellectual rigour and ruthlessness to demolishing others' arguments. Possessing a voracious capacity for hard work, he rose early, worked assiduously until lunchtime, took an afternoon stroll and then returned to his work till late in the night when he might permit himself a little relaxation – by reading economic papers.

Whilst passionate about his own policies and vision, he was not a charismatic leader and he lacked the common touch – not for him the public displays of oratory demonstrated by his contemporaries Hitler or Mussolini. Salazar's first biographer, Egerton, reports a significant yet typical response by a crowd in 1941:

Chapter 3

"As they passed the building of the Ministry of Finance, they looked up at Salazar, and their faces expressed confidence rather than enthusiasm, reverence rather than blind devotion."[2]

In the same way that Salazar rose to become leader of the government, his graduate studies flat-mate at the University of Coimbra, Manuel Cerejeira, rose to be a Cardinal and leader of the Church in Portugal. This lifelong friend summarised the baffling contradictions he saw as follows:

"Salazar walked on a straight road, oblivious of side turnings. He was a man for great issues, also for small detail. In his youth he had already developed tenacity of will, high intelligence and absolute calm. Those of us who knew him recall his rare capacity for objectivity in discussion. He had the art of outlining a theme with fine irony, but was scornful of eloquence. Now, as then, he starts a thing with a timid gesture, hesitates before committing himself, needs to feel he is supported. But then he throws himself into action. I have never observed such contrasts in a man. He appreciates the company of women and their beauty, yet leads the life of a monk. Scepticism and zest, pride and modesty, distrust and confidence, the most disarming kindness and at times the most unexpected hardness of heart – all are in constant conflict within him."[3]

Estado Novo

In 1926, Portugal embraced fully the Estado Novo [New State] through a coup d'état which overthrew the remnants of what had become a chaotic First Republic (described in Chapter 2). Like this Republic, rather than having a clear set of positive values, for many citizens it

---

[2] Egerton FCC. (1943). *Salazar: Rebuilder of Portugal.* London: Hodder & Stoughton.

[3] Described in: D'Assac P D'A. (1967). *Salazar.* Paris: La Table Ronde.

26

was easier to see what the new authoritarian regime stood *against* and some historians[4] argue that it did not have a fully-developed ideology. The movement was repulsed by Communism, liberalism, socialism and any anti-colonial views – and this was to prove a cause of much tension as Portugal's former colonies actively sought independence in the 1960s. By contrast, the Estado Novo embraced a totalitarian view of life. It was conservative, nationalistic and underpinned by strict adherence to Roman Catholic doctrine. It was the moral certainties of this faith, eschewing the shades of grey tolerated by other faiths, which Salazar sought to translate into the nation's psyche and heart. To support his aims, the secret police force, the PVDE (Polícia de Vigilância e de Defesa do Estado / State Defence and Surveillance Police) was created. This body, modelled on the Gestapo, ensured that citizens adhered to the script, in much the same way that writers like Kafka[5] and Orwell[6] were to describe later of fictional, totalitarian regimes.

The regime's fascist-leaning approach instilled a sense of order into the chaos and, at last, gave a glimpse of economic stability. It was this precious, hard-won quality which Salazar clung to and which dictated his own policies for his entire premiership, in particular his fear of destabilising the country through engagement in war. Whilst on the face of it there might be similarities with Fascist states in Europe at the time (and indeed, Salazar was reputed[7] to have a photograph of Mussolini on his desk to provide inspiration), there were distinct differences from other regimes. The Estado Novo was neither racist nor anti-Semitic; it was paternalistic in its view; and no other European political movement was so intricately entwined with a religious faith. It was also an inward-looking state, again in contrast to the European Fascist regimes. Indeed, Salazar had no taste for internationalism – he was disdainful of organisations like the League of Nations (as he would

---

[4] Wilsford D. (1995). Ibid.

[5] *The Trial*, 1914 (but incomplete)

[6] *Animal Farm* (1945) *and 1984* (1949)

[7] Lochery N. Lisbon: *War in the Shadows of the City of Light, 1939-1945*. New York: Public Affairs. p14.

be in the future to its successor, the United Nations), and of international movements or theories like Communism.

Financial saviour?

Entering government in April 1928, first as Finance Minister, Salazar believed that economic prosperity could only be achieved through tough, centralist control, resisting any attempts at modernisation and ensuring that traditional ways of life and values continued unsullied.

Certainly he displayed a rare financial ability, and maintained close control of the nation's finances, even after election as Prime Minister in 1932. In the eleven years before he took office, the nation's deficits totalled 2,574,000 contos (one conto equated to a thousand escudos, the currency of the time). Salazar believed fervently that the books must always balance and he espoused the virtues of thrift, hard work and patience. In the first eleven years of his financial ministry (between 1928 and 1939), not only did he wipe out this enormous deficit, but created a surplus of

Figure 13. Salazar, the young Minister of Finance, reading.

1,963,000 contos (at that time equivalent to about £20 million). What he would make today of the spending of EU money by the island of Madeira on a football stadium to celebrate the local hero, Cristiano Ronaldo, can only be surmised.

During the 1930s, the focus was on economic growth by building up basic services and infrastructure that would make expansion possible.

These motives were not simply financial – they were also doctrinal in keeping the populace engaged in traditional industry and agriculture.

By 1937, Salazar's achievements in economic management included developing some of the infrastructure of the country. In order of expenditure, the top three investment areas were physical improvements (particularly ports, roads, irrigation and hospitals), followed by defence, and then repayment of the national debt. In particular, he invested in irrigation and hydro-electric projects. The Portuguese population was, for a large part, too uneducated to assume anything other than that the government knew what it was doing. One of the quirks of his term in office was that he did not invest sufficiently in education, leaving many citizens unable to read or write. Kay contends[8] that the 50% illiteracy rate remained because the dictator earnestly believed that his people needed to be 'cradled' for a long time before they were able to truly benefit from such liberating concepts as literacy, education and democracy. He felt the whole weight of the nation's heritage on his shoulders and was disinclined to share that burden with lesser mortals.

Dealing with dissenters

To translate his vision into reality, Salazar needed assistance from others – the military, the Church, and the secret police force he had established as Prime Minister in 1933. The 2,000 staff of the PVDE ensured that citizens toed the line. Adherence to religious doctrine was enforced in schools; and armed service personnel were required to swear allegiance to the Estado Novo and were banned from marrying non-Catholics.[9] Communities were actively encouraged to advise the PVDE (or their 10,000 part-time informers) of any non-conformist activity in their neighbours and families. The media was strictly censored, the PVDE was used to keep left wing, dissident groups under control and many opponents were interned in prison camps on the Azores and Cape Verde Islands. Salazar summed up the character of his citizens thus:

---

[8] Kay H. (1970) *Salazar and Modern Portugal*. p72. New York: Hawthorn.

[9] Birmingham D. (2003). *A Concise History of Portugal* (2nd ed.). Cambridge: Cambridge University Press. p168.

Chapter 3

"The Portuguese peasant is religious and will remain so despite the ravages caused in his mind by the scandalous anti-clerical republic. On the other hand he is superstitious with a superstition which survives from an old paganism sometimes related to devil worship. He is sober when he has not too much money to spend, and he lives simply with few wants. With the exception of a few large landowners he is poor but does not complain. The Portuguese peasant has an air of contentment, if not of happiness, which it is a pleasure to behold. He is extremely easy to govern."[10]

There is no question that the dictator was shaped by a perspective which seems at odds with today's more open, materialistic world. For the devout Salazar, there was a tension between the attainment of a religious 'grace' through suffering and, set against this, the belief that it was man's right to share in the decisions that shape his life. He believed that there could be social solutions to social problems and that salvation might be achieved through attaining social justice in the world. This complex, at times seemingly contradictory perspective, was underpinned by a Vatican encyclical, *Rerum Novarum*, (*'Of revolutionary change'* in English) published shortly after Salazar's birth – and he appears to have almost adopted this as his childhood mantra.

Salazar's handling of the wolfram question will be uncovered in a following chapter. Suffice it to say, here, that whilst he disapproved of some espionage actions, he supported the work of the PVDE. Indeed, he felt that a crucial role of the police force was to eradicate terrorist or extremist citizens (some of whom simply took exception to his Estado Novo policies), and felt that it was justifiable to mete out 'a little rough handling' .... to make an example .... 'of such wretches'.[11] Part of the leader's deception of his own people was to misrepresent the power and influence of Portugal globally. As we have seen, Portugal was an influential country, punching above its weight in international

---

[10] Georgel J. (1981) *Le Salazarisme: Historie et Bilan, 1926-1974*. Paris: Cujas. Quoted in translation by Birmingham (2003), Op Cit.

[11] Ferro A. (1939). *Salazar, Portugal and her Leader*. London: Faber & Faber. p185

discovery and trade, yet wedded to the past. Estado Novo propaganda of the 1930s included a map of how citizens should not consider Portugal to be a small country but a large and influential one. Created in 1934, this map was on the wall of every schoolroom. It extolled the power and influence of Portugal and its African colonies by purporting to show that with its two principal African colonies – Angola and Mozambique – superimposed on a map of Europe, it was too significant a power to ignore.

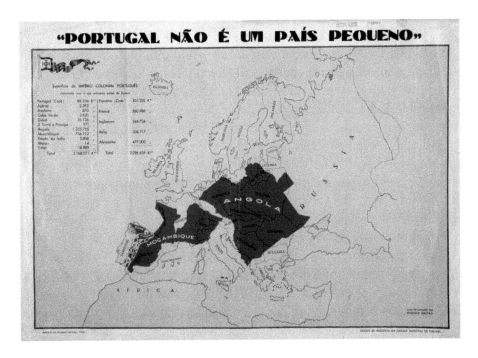

Figure 14. 'Portugal is not a small country' by Henrique Galvão. This propaganda map of 1934 shows Portuguese territories like Angola and Mozambique superimposed over Europe.

Despite his draconian rule, by the outbreak of the Second World War, Salazar's reputation was riding high internationally and Portugal had come through the world depression relatively unscathed. The controversy over his *economic* policies belongs to the post-1945 era.

Lacking charisma and a rhetoric which reached out to ordinary people, combined with his distaste for the trappings of power, Salazar was inevitably low-profile. Other international leaders may have found it difficult to understand the forces which drove him, as all they saw was a difficult man, obstinate and unbending, invoking the heritage of the state and the Church in getting his way. And yet this is something of an over-simplification because the underpinning principles of his attitude towards wartime neutrality, the wolfram question and the Azores question were deeply-rooted in the political state which he developed, as we shall see.

The Azores – a thorny problem for Salazar and the Allies

One area which marks out Salazar is his view on the Azores, that archipelago of islands off the West African coast which today is seen either as a staging post for transatlantic solo sailors or as a remote, beautiful holiday destination. Therein lies its charm and also its strategic importance. A glance at a globe reinforces the huge expanse of the Atlantic Ocean compared with the land masses either side. Being two-thirds of the way between New York and Lisbon, the Azores provide that vital stopping-off point, be it as shelter from adverse weather, for re-stocking with supplies or, in the case of air and sea-transport in the earlier decades of the twentieth century, a re-fuelling stop. Additionally, given the wartime U-boat threat in the North Atlantic, the British viewed the Azores as a potential base for Allied submarines – and feared the threat of Germany invading and creating a U-boat base there. When the United States joined the conflict, they saw the Azores as a vital staging post for transporting supplies, equipment or personnel to Europe and as an ideal static 'aircraft carrier' for military planes. Its location in more temperate waters than the alternative northern routes (which incurred greater U-boat threats, possible icebergs, and greater cost in fuel and time) made it uniquely attractive.

Salazar, however, had other ideas. His ardent Estado Novo view of neutrality meant that there should be no foreign military presence in Portuguese territory *anywhere*. Nevertheless, he was astute in recognising that he needed what Peters and Waterman were to define later in the business world as 'simultaneous loose-tight properties'[12] – in other words, core values to be closely embraced but with a variety of elastic strategies which allowed flexible interpretation when responding to changing conditions where necessary.

The British had suggested to Salazar in 1941 that, in the event of a Nazi invasion of Portugal, his government should decamp to the Azores. By 1943, both Churchill and Roosevelt were convinced of the vital role which the archipelago could play as a staging-post. The Americans had adopted a rather gung-ho approach to the potential use of the Azores which had alienated Salazar, whose preference was to deal with the British. Nevertheless, he agreed in negotiations in July 1943 to the Allies' use of the islands' military facilities, provided that it was done in a low-key manner so that Portugal could be seen internationally as external to the war. Churchill decided that this was best done under the auspices of the old Anglo-Portuguese Alliance, a decision which caused friction with Washington. Despite this, a positive outcome was reached with agreement by Portugal that Pan Am could use the islands as a refuelling point for their commercial aircraft between the US and the UK – this would also have ramifications for flights into Portugal by Pan Am as we'll see in a later chapter.

By October 1943, British forces had arrived on the Azores to use the military facilities although, as the agreement did not extend to the Allies generally, the US felt wounded. Salazar had been afraid that any concession would have granted the US permanent access to the islands which, in his narrow world-view, he was not prepared to concede. With Churchill's support, a delegation to Salazar eventually extracted from him an agreement that both British and US military personnel could use the facilities (under British supervision), provided that Americans wore both British and US insignia, with the US insignia being smaller. Such was the tricky nature of negotiation with Salazar.[13]

---

[12] Peters T & Waterman R Jr. 1982. *In Search of Excellence: Lessons from America's Best-Run Companies.* New York: HarperCollins.

[13] Lochery N. 2011. Ibid.

Chapter 3

An altered viewpoint

By 1943, the Allies felt that a turning-point had come in the conflict and that events were moving in their favour. They argued that the time had come for neutral Portugal to fully back the Allies' cause and that, post-war, such action would be rewarded. The British gained the support of the Portuguese Ambassador to London, Armindo Monteiro, who sent a closely-argued typed letter to Salazar, decrying his foreign policy and arguing for him to side openly with the Allies. As Lochery observes, Monteiro's twenty-page letter amounts to the longest political suicide note in history[14] and, not surprisingly, he was recalled and spent his future in relative obscurity. Salazar's response was revealing not just in content but also in manner. Not only did he decry the views expressed by Monteiro, he attacked his superior tone. Tellingly, Salazar hand-wrote his response on top of Monteiro's typed text so that future historians could clearly see the point-by-point repudiation of the ambassador's argument. As an accomplished academic, he thus ensured that the evidence could not be ignored.

Salazar and General Franco of Spain

Salazar's ongoing relationship with his neighbouring dictator, General Franco, was a significant diplomatic achievement. During the Spanish Civil War, Salazar was terrified of the widespread Communist ideas in Spain, fearing that they would spill across the border into his own righteous, God-fearing country. Consequently, in 1938, he formally recognised Franco's Fascist government. Just a year later, as the Second World War erupted, Salazar again feared Spain being drawn into war by capitulating to the Nazis, as it would effectively bring the Axis powers right up to the Portuguese border.

Salazar's determination to align himself with his Iberian neighbour was based on several factors. For many years, the Portuguese had felt that Spaniards stereotyped them as Iberians with their backs to Europe and their eyes set on the ocean. Salazar sought to overcome this and saw Iberia generally (as well as the Anglo-Portuguese Alliance) as guardians against Communism. Even later in the conflict, Salazar was

---

[14] Lochery N. 2011. Ibid, p181.

distrustful of the 'godless' nature of the Soviet allies and the influence they would have over traditional European values. Much as he disliked the Third Reich, at least it was anti-Communist.

The 1939 Iberian Pact was signed to ensure neutrality, although Salazar never fully trusted Franco not to go back on this agreement, given his own past support for and from Germany. As Prime Minister, he was always convinced that Portugal would have been subsumed into Spain long ago if it had not been for the Anglo-Portuguese Treaty, so the Pact was another means of retaining independence. Despite Salazar's uneasiness about the relationship, he was highly-praised by Franco, who described him as the most complete statesman, and the leader most worthy of respect that he had ever known.[15]

Salazar's ultimate impact on the war

So, how do we summarise this complex individual? Was he a world leader of stature or merely an efficient national manager? He made mistakes certainly – his aloofness meant that he did not connect with ordinary people whether in Portugal or its colonies. By the end of his tenure, his view of politics was certainly out of kilter with the democratic impulses of the day. He was 'brought to power' rather than 'swept to power' because of his financial acumen, possessing a skills-match badly needed by the Portugal of his early ministerial days. Today, the Estado Novo is all but gone in Portugal (other than as a term used for architecture of the period), although the country retains some problems as we'll see in Chapter 10. As his biographer, Hugh Kay, acknowledges[16], Salazar formed judgements and stuck with them. Whatever means he used to establish these views, he was usually unshakeable once they were formed – even if the world around him was changing. The Azores diplomatic incident marked one of the rare occasions when Salazar changed his mind – but only slightly, without compromising his principles and for the benefit of his own nation. As suggested by one US politician[17], Salazar "and his whole country were

---

[15] Preston P. (1994). *Franco: A Biography*. London: Basic Books. p454.

[16] Kay H. (1970). Ibid. p123.

[17] Ball G W. (1968). *The Discipline of Power*. Boston, Mass.: Little, Brown.

living in more than one century" – which is maybe a polite way of saying that he lived in the past.

Since his death, Salazar has been criticised for the shortcomings of the Estado Novo, the brutal repression of dissidents, his narrow world-view and his distrust of colleagues, allies, and even of the Church's representatives. Other analysts point to his clear sense of national vision, the canny manner in which he held the country together, keeping it out of war and balancing the state's books. What is clear is that he played a very shrewd game during the Second World War and kept to the spirit of neutrality.

Was Salazar truly a global leader, espousing the qualities of other great national leaders? It is difficult to ascertain the real sense of leadership he gave when, throughout the 1930s and the war years, he was always in the shadow of larger-than-life leaders like Hitler and Mussolini, each of whom established a political and military infrastructure to project their wider European vision. Whilst Salazar was a shrewd economist, the breadth and depth of his view was much more circumspect. He was passionately devoted to Portugal and to the Estado Novo as a way of maintaining both stability and the cultural heritage of the nation. Yet he was also limited by this perspective and he became afraid of the prospect of Portugal diluting its character and power. Whilst he felt that it was acceptable for Portugal to adopt a 'civilising', crusading, imperial manner over subjugated colonies, it was not acceptable for his beloved nation's traditions to be compromised. Additionally, as we will see in Chapter 4, whilst he was tolerant of refugees entering Portugal to escape tyranny, persecution or worse in their own countries, he was also ambivalent about 'the Jewish question'. He regarded this very much as an internal German matter rather than one of international concern. Is such a narrow world-view compatible with the term 'world leader' whereby national leaders express views on international matters even if they do not impact directly on their own nation?

Whilst Portugal was no longer a monarchy, a strong sense of hierarchical power continued to exist, particularly through Salazar's embracing of the power of the church. His sincerely held religious beliefs may explain some of the shortcomings and weaknesses of his administration which appear so apparent with hindsight. Why deliberately leave the people uneducated and illiterate? Why not devise a strategy for sustaining the short-lived riches afforded by wolfram?

Why not use the enormous wealth gained as a result of wartime neutrality for the benefit of the people? Why not recognise, along with other imperial nations, the right of self-determination to former colonies?

Peter Drucker, the Austro-American management writer, argues that 'management is doing things right; leadership is doing the right things.'[18] An over-simplification though this is, it neatly summarises the dichotomy which historians have encountered in evaluating Salazar's rule. Some contemporary British politicians like Foreign Secretary Anthony Eden (who had a sound grasp of Iberian matters) found his 'conduct incomprehensible in an ally'[19] and Churchill found him 'intolerable'.[20] Some post-1970s observers struggle with his world viewpoint (or lack of it) and his tolerance of the thuggery of the PVDE. Others (such as Kay[21]) consider that Salazar did Portugal proud in his deft handling of issues during the Second World War.

What is certain is that Salazar's canny orchestration of the Allies and the Axis forces – in playing one power off against another – maintained political stability, generated wealth and laid the foundations for a more optimistic future of his country. However, as we shall see in Chapter 7, these achievements were also fraught with difficulty and enduring social problems, particularly in relation to the regions where wolfram was mined.

---

[18] Drucker P F. (2003). *The Essential Drucker*. New York: Harper Business Books.

[19] Kay H. (1970). Ibid p179.

[20] Kay H. (1970.) Ibid. p181

[21] Kay H. (1970). Ibid. p181.

Chapter 4
The Lure of Lisbon

Contrasts and contradictions

A visitor to Lisbon in the 21st Century will find a charming city with many architectural, cultural and leisure attractions. Built on several hills rising steeply from the north bank of the River Tagus, Lisbon has spacious open squares and parks interspersed with narrow, cobbled streets criss-crossed by iconic, century-old electric trams. It is a city which blends an historical centre with the modern Expo pavilions upstream on the river bank. Look down from Castle Sao Jorge over the glistening River Tagus and it is apparent what a thriving international port it is, a fact celebrated down-river at Belém by the imposing monument to the *Descobrimentos*, the navigators whose discoveries in the New World in the 15th and 16th centuries brought fame, wealth and influence to the capital of this small country.

In the run-up to the Second World War, while its appeal remained strong, Lisbon was a city with different facets – from glamorous opulence to shady intrigue, as we shall see later. Like many other post-depression cities across Europe, Lisbon remained a city of poverty for many, where poor housing and disease made anything more elevated than mere survival a real challenge. Yet at the same time, just as pre-war Berlin had become a decadent European hotspot, full of lively jazz, drama and sizzling nightclubs, so Lisbon also exhibited some of this notoriety.

Berlin had attracted the intelligentsia and bohemian, creative writers such as Stephen Spender, W H Auden and Christopher Isherwood (whose novel *Goodbye to Berlin* gave rise to the musical *Cabaret*), all in search of personal and sexual freedom. From 1933, the Nazi state had its headquarters in Berlin and its powerful, imposing new architecture by Albert Speer projected unmistakably the collective Nazi vision, embodied in Berlin's Olympic Stadium.

Chapter 4

Lisbon could not emulate this, either politically through its isolationist dictator Dr Salazar, or architecturally. Nevertheless, after war broke out, the city became the default haunt for many socialites, offering a delightful climate, fashionable restaurants and shops, which sported menus and merchandise not available in ration-book countries. Demand grew not just from tourists – the country's neutrality, its strategic position on the Atlantic shipping lanes, and its welcome to many displaced European celebrities and royalty ensured that it had a magnetic attraction – in the short-term at least. A telling description of the city at this time is by the French aristocratic writer and flying pioneer, Antoine de Saint-Exupéry. Seeking escape from his homeland, which had fallen to the Nazis, de Saint-Exupéry was desperate to return to air combat for the Allies. Escaping to Lisbon, he waited there for a visa for the US and wrote, *"In 1940 Lisbon, happiness was staged so that God could believe it still existed."*[1]

Secret agents

Just down-river from Lisbon, in Estoril, lay the fashionable casino and hotels, presenting a comparable lifestyle to 1930s Berlin, minus the excesses. Providing a tantalising glimpse of wealth, no matter how transitory, the bright lights of the casino attracted many socialites as the must-be-seen-in venue. Hotels actually expanded in the early part of the war to cater for the increase in trade, although not all guests were pleasure-seekers. The number of exiled business people expanded considerably after the USA became a belligerent in 1941.

As such, Estoril attracted considerable patronage by secret agents, as we will see in detail in the next chapter.

---

[1] Katrandjian O. Quoted from unnamed document in *To Spy in Lisbon*. *Huffington Post*. 02.03.2014.

Figure 15. Palácio Hotel.

The British Royal connection

Amongst the list of major socialites was the Duke of Windsor, who had abdicated the British throne as King Edward VIII in 1936 in order to marry divorcee Wallis Simpson. The British royal family and government found the Duke an irritant – but what could they do with him? He was considered to have brought disgrace on the British establishment and was something of a loose cannon, and his lack of wisdom and discretion made him a potential liability, even after abdication. Living in considerable style on the French Riviera and with expensive tastes (courtesy of the British taxpayer), in 1937 the Windsors made a much-publicised visit to Hitler's Germany on the pretext of inspecting labour conditions. This was something in which the Duke had long been interested since his visit to Wales early in his reign when he had shown sympathy with unemployed Welsh miners. Not surprisingly, his views were represented as being full of admiration for efficient German production techniques and, rightly or wrongly, the pro-Nazi label stuck. Upon the outbreak of the Second World War, the Duke promptly offered his services to his estranged government and family, an offer which caused some disquiet given his previous record in placing personal gratification above any sense of national duty.

Chapter 4

Figure 16. The Duke of Windsor inspecting German troops on his post-abdication visit to Germany; October, 1937.

After some hesitation, the Duke of Windsor was given the job of liaison officer between the British and French high commands in France. After the fall of France, he travelled with his wife first to Spain and then on to Portugal. Whilst in Iberia in the summer of 1940 he was the subject of much Nazi interest. The Nazis had convinced themselves that the Duke was sympathetic to Germany and the German Foreign Minister – von Ribbentrop – hatched a shadowy plot called Operation Willi through which they hoped to use the Duke to overthrow the British government. There is evidence[2] of much plotting by the Germans to detain the Duke in Spain rather than allowing him to proceed to Portugal and risk destabilising the Reich's relationship with Salazar. The Germans even placed some 50 million Swiss francs at his disposal to sweeten the enticement.

However, the Windsors did travel to Portugal and stayed in the fashionable resort of Cascais on the Lisbon Riviera as guests of the

---

[2] See Lochery N. 2011. *Lisbon: War in the Shadows of the City of Light, 1939-1945*. Public Affairs: New York. Chap 11.

head of the mighty eponymous bank, Ricardo Espírito Santo. Whilst there, the Duke received a summons from Prime Minister Churchill to return to London. Annoyed at such treatment, he stayed on to maximise (some might say, to milk) the hospitality of the banker and waited to see if there was a better deal on offer. It appears that, through British agents in Lisbon, Churchill was well aware of the German plot. Concerned about what a disgruntled Duke might say to his host (who in turn had the ear of Salazar), an offer was made for him to become Governor of the Bahamas. Clearly, the title, the prestige, and the climate appealed to the Windsors and they set sail on 1 August 1940, safely out of the way for the rest of the war of both the British government and potential Nazi intervention.

Escape from Lisbon

Wartime socialites with a less secure exit route included many who had already made a perilous journey to Lisbon. Why did they come here? In the famous wartime film *Casablanca*, the Humphrey Bogart character, Rick, warns Ilsa that she must board the plane from Casablanca to Lisbon. If she does not, she will regret it "Maybe not today, maybe not tomorrow, but soon and for the rest of your life." No doubt this sentiment was shared by many other escapees, whose travels were more tortuous and less lovelorn. Lisbon's neutrality and coastal location made it an ideal stopping off point for onward travel to other safe havens. Arthur Koestler, en route to England, described Lisbon as being "the last open gate of a concentration camp."[3]

In particular, Lisbon was a popular escape routes for Jews as their persecution by the Nazis spread across many European countries. For many centuries, Lisbon had embraced a Jewish population and a new synagogue had been established in 1904. Although Salazar had, from 1929, introduced an austere form of nationalism, it was not based on any biological or racial theory, so the number of Jews emigrating from punitive dictatorships in central Europe increased. Many made it by train, by car, or even on foot through France and Spain. Indeed, the

---

[3] Kaplan, M. 2013. *Lisbon is Sold Out! The Daily Lives of Jewish Refugees in Portugal During World War II*. New York. Tikvah Center for Law and Jewish Civilization.

Chapter 4

number of Jews granted residential visas for Portugal rose from 400 to over one thousand on the outbreak of war and this number was to rise phenomenally[4] as living conditions for Jews in other countries deteriorated. The report by the Portuguese secret police (PVDE) for 1940 alone indicated that a total of 43,540 refugees had arrived in Portugal (30,854 by land, 6,800 by sea and 5,840 by air). The total number of exits were 36,000, leaving 6,000 still in Portugal – waiting for exit visas, sufficient funds or a definite onward destination.

What were the escape routes from Lisbon? For most Jews, it was to the United States, still a long and potentially hazardous sea-journey away. Called 'the Bottleneck of Europe'[5], the quayside in Lisbon was regularly a frantic scene of activity as unwashed, poorly-dressed refugees queued to gain a place on the weekly ship to New York. Desperately clutching their exit papers along with their few possessions, their departure (if successful), would free up room for new waves of refugees. Every hotel room in Lisbon, along the coastal strip and the surrounding villages was filled. The Jewish diaspora was strong in the US, particularly on the eastern seaboard. An emerging destination for Jews was also Palestine, although the state of Israel was yet to be established.

For some more wealthy escapees, flights to the USA were an option. These would have been virtually impossible without Salazar granting the use of the Azores archipelago from 1943 as a refuelling stop, given that the islands occupied a strategic point in the eastern Atlantic. As mentioned in Chapter 3, the relationship between Churchill and Roosevelt as Allies, and Salazar as neutral dictator, was testy and it took considerable negotiation and patience to get Salazar to agree to the Allies' military use of the Azores (known as Operation Lifebelt). It is, indeed, one of the lesser-known agreements of the war which made a significant difference to the Allied side – transatlantic flights were

---

[4] Figures taken from Lochery N. University College London lunch-time lecture, 28 January 2011. *Lisbon 1939-1945: the untold story of Portugal and the Jewish Refugees.* Available on: https://www.youtube.com/watch?v=Kr9sdiZOCQc#t=48

[5] Bayles W D. Lisbon: Europe's Bottleneck. New York: *Life* Magazine. 26 April 1941.

more secure and the routes from Europe to Africa and South America became more controlled. For wealthy refugees, the prospect of a luxurious flight aboard a Pan-Am Yankee Clipper (a flying boat which landed in the River Tagus) was most appealing. It would provide almost a magic carpet, regular twice-weekly flight between Lisbon and New York and was a much talked-of and hoped-for escape. For those who achieved this ambition, the fear, deprivation and persecution of the old world was left behind as the Clipper took off from the estuary, soon reaching the wide Atlantic beyond Cascais.

Two factors prevented this option becoming a reality for many. Firstly, the cost. For many refugees, even scraping together the fares for a sea-passage was an enormous burden. For some refugees, the process could take not just weeks, but months or even years. To think of upgrading the cost to an airfare was simply an unattainable dream when one's life predominantly involved seeking food, shelter and travel visas. All the time they would be living in fear not only of discovery by German-leaning spies or informers, but exploitation by local residents trying to enhance their own meagre incomes by any means. Unable to secure gainful employment to supplement their precious savings, for some escapees the only way to raise funds was via prostitution, in competition with the locals. It is reported[6] that during the Second World War, the incidence of venereal disease in Lisbon reached epidemic proportions.

The second factor was the fatal crash of a Yankee Clipper in the Tagus on 22 February, 1943. The plane had thirty-nine passengers and crew aboard, of whom twenty-four died either as a result of the impact or drowning in the freezing river. Foul play was not suspected, but questions were asked about the angle of descent, the direction of the plane and, particularly, about the wisdom of landing in darkness on a river. The result was that Clipper flights to New York were suspended for some time after the accident and it clearly had an impact on the willingness of wealthy refugees to use such a service. Instead they joined (or jumped?) the queue for a sea-passage.

---

[6] Brandao F N. Epidemiology of Venereal Disease in Portugal during the Second World War. *British Journal of Venereal Diseases*. 36, no. 2 (1960). p136.

Figure 17. Boeing 314 Yankee Clipper on River Tagus.

Celebrities

So, who were some of the other wealthy, famous or socialite refugees? 1930s Estoril, just a short train ride along the Tagus estuary from Lisbon, had become the adopted home for many exiled European royalty and aristocrats. Titled exiles included the Spanish royal family, King Carol II of Romania, King Umberto of Italy, the Empress Zita of Hapsburg, Regent Horthy of Hungary, Great Duchess Charlotte of Luxembourg, the Danish royal family, and Count Henri, pretender to the throne of France. Estoril offered the nearest they could find to high-society and a tolerance for their former way of life.

Refugees from the arts world included the filmmaker Max Ophuls (who found obtaining the transit visas "infernally difficult to get"[7]) and the Belgian Nobel laureate Maurice Maeterlinck. The *New York Times* quoted him[8] as saying:

---

[7] Bacher L. 1996. *Max Ophuls in the Hollywood Studios*. New Jersey: Rutgers University Press.

[8] Knapp B. 1975. *Maurice Maeterlinck*. Boston: Thackery Publishers. p18.

"I knew that if I was captured by the Germans I would be shot at once, since I have always been counted as an enemy of Germany because of my play, The Mayor of Stilmonde, which dealt with the conditions in Belgium during the German Occupation of 1918."

Other refugees included the famous writer and naturalised British subject Arthur Koestler; 'undesirable foreigner' Max Ernst; the Surrealist painter Marc Chagall, described by Australian art critic Robert Hughes as the "quintessential 20th century Jewish artist"; German-Jewish pacifist journalist Berthold Jacob and the gay, Czech / German historian Golo Mann (son of author Thomas Mann).

Whilst Estoril became the last resort (literally) of displaced royalty and aristocracy, very few of those passing through – in the early years of the war – decided to stay. Figures vary but several hundred thousand refugees are estimated to have arrived in the nation during the hostilities. One of these was the Armenian oil magnate Calouste Gulbenkian, who was known as 'Mr Five Per Cent' for his habit of retaining a 5% stake in the oil companies he developed. Gulbenkian amassed not only a huge fortune but also a huge art collection, which he left on his death in 1955 to the Portuguese people. Lisbon is still the headquarters today of both the Calouste Gulbenkian Foundation (which devotes itself to charitable work in the sphere of the arts, education and science) and the Gulbenkian Art Museum.

Whilst not a refugee, the celebrated economist John Maynard Keynes passed through Estoril en-route in 1941 to meetings in the US from which would emerge in 1944 the Bretton Woods agreement on the post-war financial system based upon Keynesianism. In total, the Cascais Military Police alone recorded over twenty-thousand foreign nationals passing through the Estoril area from 1939 onwards during the war; many of whose names have passed into history.[9]

---

[9] The Post Office in Estoril, itself a fine example of Estado Novo architecture from 1942, now houses a fascinating, permanent exhibition entitled 'Espaço Memória dos Exílios Estoril'. Many of the exhibits have been loaned from the Palácio Hotel across the road.

Chapter 4

Escape into Portugal

Not all refugees were able to embrace the happiness noted by Antoine de Saint-Exupéry. In many cases, they were either of Jewish ethnicity or artists who supported forms of art very much frowned on by the Nazis. In the case of Peggy Guggenheim, her list of 'undesirable' activities was added to by building up a collection of artwork much sought-after by the Nazis who had started to raid much of Europe for art treasures.

For many refugees, assistance for their plight came from a variety of Jewish relief committees who were active in Portugal. It is difficult to estimate the total number who found assistance with financial support, clothing, food, shelter, visas and onward passage but it certainly runs to many, many thousands. Relief work was also assisted by the unlikely intervention of a non-Jew, Aristides de Sousa Mendes, the Portuguese Consul in Bordeaux. After the fall of France, the unofficial, temporary capital of France had been transferred to Bordeaux, so his role was very important. Located in the south-west of France and with tidal access though its great river port, Bordeaux was also the last chance for any refugees fleeing from northern France. If they could not be shipped safely out of Bordeaux in time, they were likely to find themselves heading to a concentration camp. One man assisted by de Sousa Mendes was Rabbi Chaim Kruger. Polish by birth but a resident of Brussels, Kruger refused to accept the visa offered by de Sousa Mendes until each refugee in Bordeaux had also received one. It was this act of moral courage which spurred on de Sousa Mendes further.

Like Salazar, de Sousa Mendes was a law graduate from Coimbra University and was committed to saving Jews and non-Jews alike from the Nazi clutches. No one knows exactly how many thousands of people he saved by providing visas for safe entry into Portugal but some estimates suggest up to 10,000. In the 2007 TV poll of *Os Grandes Portugueses* (the Greatest Portuguese), de Sousa Mendes came third with 13% of the votes.[10]

*Figure 18. Aristedes de Sousa Mendes, Portuguese Consul
in Bordeaux, pictured with Rabbi Kruger.*

The mystery of Leslie Howard's disappearance

Glamorous wartime Lisbon also had a high-profile, show-business
casualty, Leslie Howard. A Hollywood star born in London, Howard
had starred in the famous movie *Gone With The Wind*, released in 1939
at the outset of the war. During the war, his fame had continued,
particularly as a key participant in British war propaganda films. It was
on behalf of the British Council that he was on a lecture tour in
Portugal and Spain, promoting the Allied cause. Howard (née Steiner)
had good reason to support this; his Jewish background made him all
too aware of the plight of Jewry across Europe.

---

[10] Beating de Sousa Mendes into first place was Salazar with 41% of the
votes. In second place was the Communist leader during the Estado Novo
period and in the aftermath of Salazar's death, Àlvaro Cunhal, with 19%.

Chapter 4

However, the Iberian tour had not gone well. Howard was in poor health and he felt that his goodwill was being exploited, and had cut short the tour, returning to Lisbon early. Foregoing his original intention of holidaying in Estoril, he aimed to get a direct return flight to the UK. It is one of the ironies of wartime life in Portugal that there remained regular BOAC flights from Lisbon to Whitchurch airport, located in a suburb of Bristol. These flights were invariably full of British officials and they could be dangerous, being tracked by the Germans, so the civilian planes were camouflaged and pilots had a variety of evasion strategies. On 31 May 1943, Howard and his agent, Alfred Chenhalls, made their way to Lisbon's Portela airport in the hope of persuading passengers to give up their seats. They were out of luck and had to return the following morning for the 09.30 flight. Flight 777A took off on-time safely, headed north across north-western Spain and out across the Bay of Biscay. However, it was spotted by the Luftwaffe and, instead of seeking cloud cover, the airliner remained visible and was shot down by a fighter plane. The BOAC pilot had managed to radio Whitchurch of the impending attack and no more was heard from the plane: no wreckage or survivors were ever found. Was it a deliberate attack? Did the plane encounter a mechanical failure? For a while, several theories existed. Capturing Howard alive would have been a propaganda victory for the Nazis. However, the confirmation by the Luftwaffe pilot of a 'kill' as he saw the airliner plunge into the sea put paid to this theory …. but not to others.

*Figure 19. Press cuttings in British Council library,
Lisbon relating to Leslie Howard's disappearance.*

Several coincidences mesh together in this tale. Howard's agent,
Chenhalls, was considered by some people to bear a striking
resemblance to Winston Churchill, particularly because of his portly
figure, bald head, and love of cigars. A photograph taken of Howard,
Chenhalls and dinner guests at the Hotel Aziz in Lisbon a day before
the flight confirms this. Could Chenhalls have been mistaken by a
German agent for Churchill on the fruitless trip to the airport for tickets
the preceding day? Churchill was actually at a summit meeting in
Casablanca at the time and was preparing to return to Britain, so it was
feasible that he had stopped off in Lisbon. As Lochery points out[11],
German intelligence knew of the trip and had ordered their aircrews to
shoot down any enemy aircraft spotted in the area in the hope of killing

---

[11] Lochery N. (2011). Ibid. p159.

Chapter 4

Churchill. It was also rumoured that Churchill's bodyguard looked rather like Howard and so there could have been a second disastrous case of mistaken identity. If this confusion had been reported to Berlin, might they have despatched a Luftwaffe patrol to the Bay of Biscay to lie in wait? Whilst this seems an intriguing possibility, would Churchill really have turned up unescorted at the airport and with no apparent secret service protection? Would he have flown on a regular commercial flight? Would he really not have been able to persuade passengers that, as Prime Minister, he had more urgent need of a seat than they did?

In fact, Churchill did make a safe night-time return flight from Casablanca, his plane making a wide sweep out into the Bay of Biscay to avoid enemy aircraft. But the matter did not rest there. Churchill was distressed by the loss of Howard and his aircraft. It later transpired that, at a critical moment in the development of the ENIGMA code-breaking operation, British intelligence actually knew that the Germans were going to attack the plane. However, cancelling the flight would have signalled to the Germans that British intelligence had intercepted their message. The flight had to take off to its doom in order to protect the lives of others who would be saved by this counter-intelligence. That would have been part of Churchill's heartache. As we now know[12], the code-breakers are considered to have shortened the war by two to three years and consequently saved millions of lives.

Furthermore, the loss of this plane brought considerable difficulties in Lisbon for the Germans. Salazar had just completed an investigation into German espionage activities in Lisbon and he was now under pressure from the British to take action against German spies. The loss of flight 777A was the last straw for Salazar and he decreed that spying by both sides in Lisbon was now a criminal offence. With the death of a glamorous screen-idol, the tide of the war was changing.

---

[12] Copeland J. http://www.bbc.co.uk/news/technology-18419691

Chapter 5
Spies, Secrets and Sex

As we saw in Chapter 3, Portugal's neutrality was a study in the pursuit of a 'pure' ideal translated into action by an unbending academic turned politician. Whilst Salazar held the nation dear in his heart, his contradictory ideals also persuaded him that his people were not yet sufficiently mature politically, educationally or economically to embrace a new world of greater wealth – one which he distrusted anyway. By the early years of the conflict, Lisbon had become a crucial piece of the war jigsaw. Many goods were processed through the port, exported to both the Allies and the Axis powers, in exchange for imported goods, currency or bullion.

In order to trade successfully and, with apparent equanimity, Salazar needed to ensure that everything went to plan. Not a man with the common touch, in order to keep himself in power he needed the secret police force which he had established to monitor the populace and keep them in check – whether it was his own citizens or the increasing number of foreign refugees and spies in wartime Lisbon. Secret police forces were by no means unusual in 1930s and 1940s Europe. Their work has been well-recorded in the works of writers such as Franz Kafka, Arthur Koestler and George Orwell. For some nations, a reliance on a secret police force would last well into the middle of the century and beyond – for example under Stalin in the USSR, the Stasi in the former East Germany and more recently in Chile, Iran, Iraq, Israel, Romania and South Africa.

The Abwehr

The Portuguese secret police force was modelled on Germany's Abwehr, although Salazar could hardly have chosen a worse model. Of the three Axis powers' secret service organisations, the Abwehr was the worst. It was poorly-organised, constantly fighting the rival SS-run organisation – the SD (Sicherheitsdienst) – and was prone to corruption. It was also the most easily-deceived of the three secret services[1], operating loosely as a set of independent cells with no centralised link. Whilst this approach might work well later for organisations such as the French Liberation bodies, the IRA or the Red Brigade (to ensure that no single cell could provide information to interrogators about other cells' activities), it was inappropriate for a centralised government intelligence service. Corruption was rife, particularly in the capital cities of neutral countries where agents were free to top-slice the movement of funds.

The Abwehr was organised into five Abteilungs (sections): Abteilung I dealt with straightforward intelligence abroad; II dealt with sabotage and controlled espionage activity; III concerned itself with counter-espionage; IV was for military attachés and open operations abroad; and V was the central section coordinating the role of all the other sections. This arrangement alone appeared to be a complex recipe for potential duplication and omission.

Additionally, the German head of the Abwehr, Admiral Canaris, could not be described as an ardent Nazi. Appointed to his position in 1935, partly because of his fluent Spanish, he had advised his friend General Franco to stay out of the war as Germany was bound to lose. Canaris filled the top echelons of the Abwehr with officers like himself – old-school patricians who were able to partially mask their ineffectiveness with charm. Being from the same 'old school tie' background as himself, they were unlikely to divulge to the Gestapo hierarchy anything less than fulsome adherence to the Nazi ideals. The Admiral was court-martialled after the attempt on Hitler's life as he was suspected of being indirectly involved and was subsequently executed. Denying that he was a traitor, but acting only out of duty to his country, Canaris was reputed to have said, "*I always believed in National Socialism but never in Hitler.*"

Portugal's Polícia de Vigilância e de Defesa do Estado (PVDE) was established in 1933 before evolving into the Polícia Internacional e de Defesa do Estado (PIDE) in 1945. It had a number of functions but was primarily intended to monitor and crush political dissent. It also

---

[1] Holt T. (2004). *The Deceivers: Allied Military Deception in the Second World War*. London: Weidenfeld & Nicholson.

supported the work of the Estado Novo (although you might be pushed to find any articulation of ideological support) and to report on any activity which did not conform to the leader's diktats. Apart from the two-thousand staff, there were also ten-thousand part-time informers. Such was the power of the police that citizens were encouraged to spy on their work colleagues, their neighbours, even their own families and to report any suspected misdemeanours to the authorities. There were stories of early-morning raids, of night-time beatings and, of course, of fractured families. The lack of trust in colleagues, friends and family created a climate which not only broke community ties but also made citizens fearful of their own welfare and lack trust in others.

The former Abwehr headquarters in Lisbon is now a luxurious, gated apartment building which it is not possible to see close-up, let alone visit. The PVDE's own base was on a steep hillside; built partly underground to obscure comings and goings, it also housed prison cells. Ironically, much of it was a former convent, linked by underground passages, originally to allow the nuns to move around within their own community. During the Salazar era, the underground cells had a different use and, linked to the courthouse, were testament to the original meaning in law of 'being sent down'. For most Lisboans and immigrants, however, the main source of fear emanated from the PVDE courthouse in Largo da Boa Hora, just up the hillside from Cais de Sodre station and close to the Praça do Municipio where the Portuguese Republic had been declared so proudly and confidently in 1910. Those political prisoners who were spared death would be despatched to various Portuguese-African colonies where tropical diseases might finish them off before the punishment and incarceration did so. By 1936, Salazar had established a concentration camp at Tarrafel in the Cape Verde Islands and, whilst the death penalty had been abolished in both Portugal and its colonies, the camp Governor told his first cohort of inmates that, "Those who come to Tarrafel come to die."

After several unsuccessful attempts by army officers to overthrow Salazar in 1937, he undertook a reform of the secret police. The Italian dictator, Mussolini, was asked to send agents to train the PVDE in torturing suspects – specifically in new techniques which would leave no visible signs.

Chapter 5

The internal PVDE (and later the PIDE) spy networks were enormous. As mentioned in Chapter 3, during the war years there were 10,000 informers (also called 'snitches'). But in peace-time there also remained many informers. Official records show that in 1974 there was a waiting list of 100,000 people hoping to be spies at the close of Salazar's rule. In a poor country, whether in peace or war, the additional income provided welcome food, shelter and some physical security, if not guilt-free emotions.

The PVDE also kept a close eye on both the German and British embassies, both of which were located in the Lampa district. Propaganda newssheets (often cartoon-based for the many semi-literate Lisboans) were available from each side's propaganda shops, written in Portuguese with each issue ensuring that relevant victories could be claimed. Every publication – newspapers, books, children's textbooks and magazines – was censored, any spare space created by the deletions of unacceptable material being replaced by propaganda fillers.

Whilst Lisbon may have gained a reputation as 'the city of lights', it was also a city of dark deeds, long shadows and shuffling, anonymous people, raincoat collars turned up and wide-brimmed trilby hats pulled down to mask facial features. These shadowy figures included agents of the PVDE keeping a watchful eye, not just on foreign spies but also their own citizens. The cafes of the Rossio district became the haunt not just of intellectuals reading the censored press in the pavement cafes, but also of those willing to exchange information for a price. We shall meet some of these individuals in the next chapter. The price and the means of payment could vary, from a few escudos for titbits to large sums of money, laundered through the myriad of banks which had proliferated in the era, none more so than that run by Ricardo Espírito Santo.

Estoril

Lisbon apart, there was the more glamorous setting of Estoril, a short train ride from Cais de Sodre station in downtown Lisbon or, equally a few miles by newly-opened highway along the coast (the 'Marginal'). It is rumoured that Salazar, whilst living in Cascais just west of Estoril, had ordered the Marginal to be built so that he could travel by road and not have to ride the public railway where he might easily be recognised.

As mentioned in Chapter 4, Estoril boasted a casino (the largest in Europe, bigger even than Monte Carlo). Depending on your point of view, this gambling opportunity attracted either the social elite or the dissolute. Whichever way, then as now, it was frequented by those with money to flaunt.

> "*Anyone today (1943) who frequents the Estoril Casino ………… has no idea of how elegant, select and amazing it was on a casino evening or night in the International Casino. A profusion of Paris gowns, jewels, plumed hats, high style and every face well-known, almost always an aristocrat and always 'very chic'.*"[2]

The favourite hotel for those visiting the casino was the Palácio, still trading successfully today as a five-star hotel, with its imposing architecture, fine cuisine, attentive staff and assorted sporting and leisure facilities. Just a stone's throw away lay the casino; whilst opposite, just across the Marginal, glistened the fine sands of Estoril beach and its view up the estuary towards Lisbon or seawards to Cascais and the Atlantic Ocean. From here you could sail south to Africa, west for the USA or northwards for Britain, Ireland and northern Europe. An estuary it might be but it was narrow enough for spies to keep an eye on the maritime traffic, bringing in goods from the Portuguese-African colonies, from across the Atlantic and from Britain – or vice versa. Wolfram was one of these commodities being despatched to both sides through ports and border crossings. Movements were closely monitored as it was crucial to have a clear sense of the timings and the volumes of such supplies. In some cases, ships were simply refuelling at the port of Lisbon, strategically located in the shipping lanes between Europe, Africa and the Americas. And handily between the Marginal road and the estuary was the railway line. From the right bedrooms in the Palácio, all these movements were in view.

---

[2] Translated from Colaco BG and Archer M. (1943). *Memórias da Linha de Cascais.* (*Memories of the Cascais Line.*) Republished 1999 by Municipal Councils of Cascais and Oeiras.

Chapter 5

Not surprisingly, The Palácio became the favourite haunt of British agents and guests, whereas the Germans favoured the adjoining Parque Hotel and also the nearby Atlântico Hotel (where the British royal couple, the Duke and Duchess of Windsor were hosted when not staying at the nearby house of Ricardo Espírito Santo). Their choice of hotel would have caused further concern to the British authorities, particularly as British agents rumbled the plans drawn up in the Atlântico by the Gestapo to kidnap the Duke at the hotel and install him as King in London once Britain was successfully defeated. Another German resident of the Atlântico was Hans Weber, whose role was to coordinate the network for smuggling wolfram. Hotel records show that he first stayed there on 7 October 1942 and was to remain associated with the hotel right up to his 1944 role in selling off German assets in Portugal.[3]

Back at the Palácio, even today the architecture and décor all convey restrained good taste – the large marble-floored lobby, the sun pouring through the west-facing floor to ceiling windows overlooking the garden and pool, the oak-panelled dining room and the array of bars. But beneath these features lies an intriguing history. In the lobby is a small display cabinet presenting the guest registration of one former guest, that of a British government official by the name of Mr Fleming. A British navy Commander, Ian Fleming had been sent to Estoril in 1941 to keep an eye on one particular agent, Colonel Popov (codename Tricycle). Further details of their relationship will be examined in Chapter 6.

Stranger even than events in a James Bond novel was the complexity of relationships between intelligence officers or secret agents. Espionage in the Palácio was legion. When the adjoining Parque Hotel was demolished, contractors found listening devices and wiring used by German spies to eavesdrop on conversations between British agents in the Palácio. So well-known was this threat that occasionally some British agents would sign off their discussion by saying farewell to their German friends. Stories abounded of the bar being host to agents watching each other's body language and trying to eavesdrop on

---

[3] Records of the Atlântico Hotel, recorded in the brochure for the Atlântico Estoril Residence, available online at:
http://www.atlanticoestorilresidence.com/downloads/brochura_en.pdf

muffled conversations. Indeed the term 'champagne spies' was used where toasts to recent victories were made – of course, these celebrations could also be false in order to throw the enemy off what had actually occurred. That the site of the Parque Hotel should have been replaced now by a luxury apartment complex run by the Palácio Hotel adds an ironic twist in European relations. Many of the apartments are apparently owned by wealthy Brazilians who feel safe in the environs of Estoril and can dispense with the bodyguards and bullet-proof cars they consider essential in today's Rio de Janeiro.[4]

The impact of double agents

Lisbon saw many spies pass through it but some were based there, including several well-established double agents – claiming to work for one side but actually reporting to the enemy as well. Of these, two were particularly important – the agents code-named Tricycle and Garbo.

Tricycle

Dusko Popov was a fun-loving Serb from Dubrovnik who had gained a law degree and doctorate from the prestigious Freiburg University in southern Germany during the 1930s, where he met fellow student 'Johnny' Jebsen. Then, as now, Freiburg was an elite university nestling in a beautiful location between the Rhine Valley and the Black Forest, from which many graduates could expect to enter high-quality jobs. Establishing his own law firm in Dubrovnik, Popov was approached in 1940 by Jebsen who confided that, since university days, he had become a researcher (or 'forscher') for the Abwehr. Popov succumbed to Jebsen's suggestion and accepted the more formal invitation from a German Embassy official to become a fellow forscher. However, he was developing a plan of his own to persuade the British Embassy in Belgrade to allow him to become a double agent. Suspecting that Popov was merely a grasping crook, the British nevertheless arranged a conversation for Popov with the British military intelligence arm, MI6, in Belgrade. Here he claimed that his heart was with the Allied cause. There was good reason to believe this – patriots in the former Yugoslavia had rebelled against the Regent,

---

[4] According to the Concierge at the Palácio, April 2015.

Chapter 5

Prince Paul, for signing a pact with Hitler. Thrown into one of his infamous furies, Hitler postponed all operations (including the invasion of Russia) in order to wreak revenge on Yugoslavia. The bloody and merciless revenge crushed the opposition (although Marshal Tito was to lead the underground movement and eventually become the nation's post-war leader) and Popov feared for the safety of his family. After the delay caused by the onslaught, Hitler was now too late to gain victory over Russia in the autumn of 1941 as he had planned. This was one of those significant occasions when the Führer placed personal rage and revenge above strategic clear thinking.

Meanwhile Jebsen made plans for Popov's cover – as an export-import businessman – between his native Yugoslavia and Britain, which necessitated frequent trips to neutral Lisbon. Tongue-in-cheek, Popov named his company Tarlair – possibly a play on the name of the head of the 'Double Cross' team in MI5 which handled double-agents ('Tar' Robertson) and their propensity to lie. His specialism as a business lawyer was in gaining Navy Certificates (Navy Certs) to authorise the shipment of goods by sea from Portugal to Yugoslavia. As long as the goods were not deemed to be part of the war effort (and thus of potential use to the Germans), such 'certs' could be granted. It took a legal mind to differentiate between goods which were combat-friendly and those destined for ordinary civilian use. Here Popov began his frequent, all-expenses paid stays at the Palácio where he would write his innocuous letters to be intercepted by the Abwehr (the blank side of the pages being covered in secret ink derived from a headache cure dissolved in white gin). And it was here that the playboy Agent Ivan (as he was known to the Abwehr) also became known to the British as Agent Tricycle because of his reported predilections for sexual threesomes.

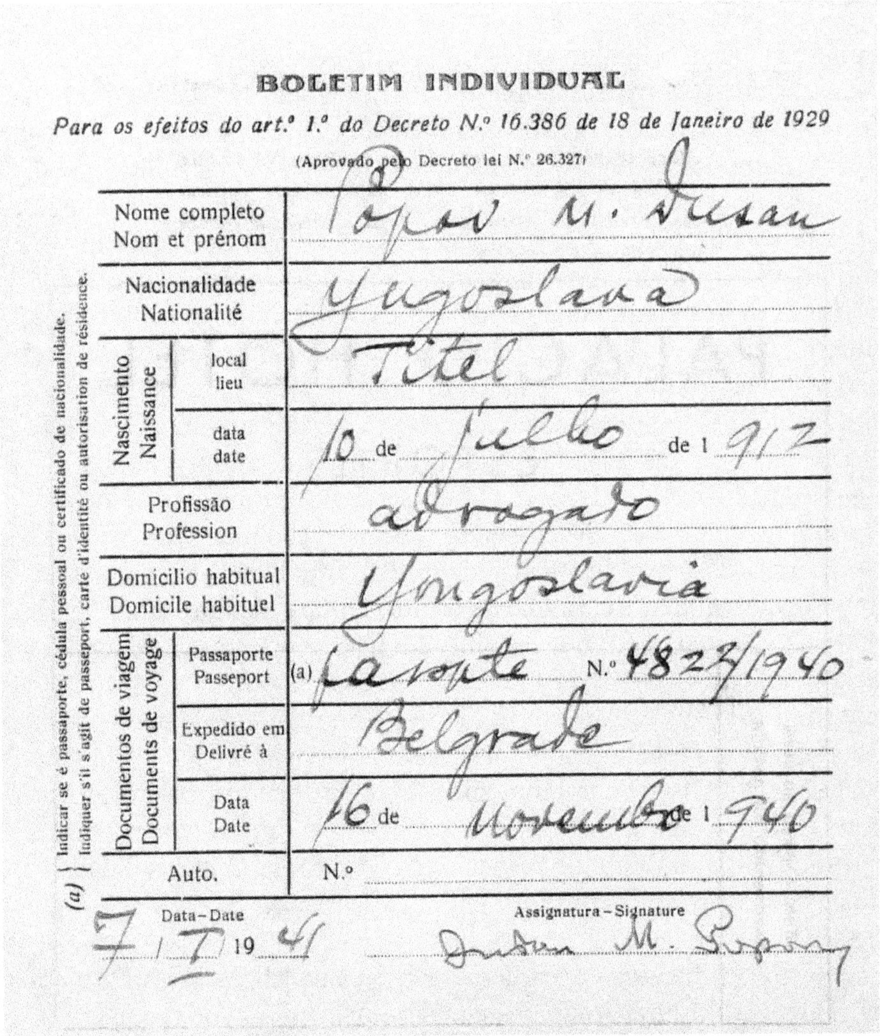

BOLETIM INDIVIDUAL

Para os efeitos do art.º 1.º do Decreto N.º 16.386 de 18 de Janeiro de 1929

(Aprovado pelo Decreto lei N.º 26.327)

Nome completo / Nom et prénom	Popov M. Dusan
Nacionalidade / Nationalité	Yugoslava
Nascimento / Naissance — local / lieu	Titel
Nascimento / Naissance — data / date	10 de Julho de 1912
Profissão / Profession	advogado
Domicilio habitual / Domicile habituel	Yougoslavia
Documentos de viagem / Documents de voyage — Passaporte / Passeport	(a) Pasaporte N.º 4827/1940
Expedido em / Delivré à	Belgrade
Data / Date	16 de Novembro de 1940
Auto.	N.º

(a) Indicar se é passaporte, cédula pessoal ou certificado de nacionalidade. / Indiquer s'il s'agit de passeport, carte d'identité ou autorisation de résidence.

Data-Date 7/I/1941

Assignatura-Signature Dusan M. Popov

Figure 20. Registration form for Dusko Popov at the Palácio Hotel.

Popov's success as an agent in Lisbon and the UK became well-established. To the Germans he became invaluable in the earlier years of the war, being described by MI6 as "the Abwehr's best agent in the UK."[5] One of Popov's key roles was to front German espionage operations in the USA, whilst simultaneously being despatched from

---

[5] British security service file KV 2/857, quoted in Macintyre. (2012). *Double Cross – The True Story of the D-Day Spies*. London: Bloomsbury. p262.

Chapter 5

Lisbon to New York by MI5 to create a network of double agents. This ambitious mission was unsuccessful, partly because the head of the Federal Bureau of Investigation (the FBI), J Edgar Hoover, took such a dislike to Popov's background and lifestyle. Whilst MI5 accepted that agents, particularly double agents, were required to be ruthless and that their need for personal secrecy prevented them from making lasting or deep personal relationships, by contrast the FBI considered such attributes to be merely symptomatic of licentious and dissolute social misfits who were temperamentally and psychologically unable to forge close relationships. That Popov was also a highly-paid, profligate and flamboyant spendthrift only added to Hoover's refusal to accept his intelligence (as Popov was to claim publicly in his autobiography) that the Japanese were likely to attack Pearl Harbor. Certainly, Popov's autobiographical reminiscences of his several meetings with Hoover present the latter as an ill-tempered, straight-laced man with no time for viewpoints other than his own and guiltless of any accusation that he was a good listener. Researchers consider Popov's claim about Pearl Harbor to be imagined[6] but certainly MI5 was very frustrated by the lack of support from the FBI as the agent carried out his mission in reporting back to the Abwehr in Lisbon. Illuminatingly, Popov refers to the stress of his role at that time, something he was unable to share with others – as "having the psychological DTs, the occupational disease of spies."[7] In due course, he returned to Lisbon, but not before racking up enormous bills for both the Abwehr and MI5 for clothing, holidays, cars and an apartment complete with man-servant.

Popov's favourite cars appear to have been Buicks. As part of the US's huge General Motors group, Buick was considered to be second only to Cadillac in the GM hierarchy of marques. Its models were considered to be refined, relatively understated and the default choice for American lawyers, doctors and other professionals. Perhaps this was the image Popov was trying to convey. In Lisbon, however, the Buick dealership in the broad, tree-lined Avenida de Liberade was also suspected of being a front for laundering Nazi gold, particularly in the

---

[6] Popov's 1974 book *Spy / Counterspy* is described by Macintyre as 'vigorously written, entertaining and partly invented' (MacIntyre, op. cit. p349), whilst Holt (op. cit. p787) describes it as 'an imaginative memoir'.

[7] Popov. Op cit. p118-119.

closing stages of the war – when Germany desperately attempted to keep its assets out of the hands of the invading Allies.

Popov had post-war aspirations to become the British Consul in Dubrovnik and to receive a decoration. Whilst he did not achieve the former, there is a wry turn of events regarding the latter. His spying career for the British had started at the Savoy Hotel in London and he had developed this skill frequenting the hotel bars of Estoril. In 1947, he was presented, by the MI5 official who had recruited him, with a leather box containing an OBE. This discreet and low-key presentation took place in the bar of the Ritz Hotel in London in recognition of Popov's role 'in deceiving the enemy prior to the Normandy invasion'. Such secretive, 'under the table operations', seemed fitting for someone who was not to reveal his identity as Agent Tricycle until thirty years after the war.

Garbo

A former chicken farmer from Barcelona, Juan Manuel Pujol became one of the most influential yet little-known double agents of WWII. Given the skills he perfected for acting his part, he was dubbed Agent Garbo after the beautiful and alluring Swedish-American screen star of the time, Greta Garbo. It was not for his looks that the agent was so dubbed, but rather for his desire to be left alone, as famously and frequently misquoted by the screen star.[8] Motivated by his experiences in the Spanish Civil War, Pujol had developed a loathing of all totalitarian regimes, be they fascist or communist (exactly like the British author George Orwell). Just as Popov had done, Pujol presented his services to the British but was turned down twice by incredulous staff. He had no history, no pedigree, no-one to vouch for him. Were they faced with a loquacious madman? It was only when London identified that the person who had been sending the Abwehr messages over some years about false movements by the Allies that they deduced that this must be one and the same person. Pujol had taken in the Germans with his preposterous stories of major British naval manoeuvres on landlocked Lake Windermere, of British diplomats

---

[8] "I never said 'I want to be alone'. I only said I wanted to be left alone. There is all the difference". Quoted in Bainbridge J. (1955). *Garbo*. NY: Doubleday.

Chapter 5

decamping to Brighton (allegedly the British equivalent of Basque coast resort San Sebastian) to escape the summer heat of London, of a non-existent convoy from Malta, and so on. Perplexed by his ability to convince the Abwehr of these stories, the Double Cross team of MI6 considered him worth interrogating and, after two weeks of intensive focus in London, they concluded that he was telling the truth and was a suitable candidate as a double-agent, whereupon he was given a cover job as a translator for the BBC.

In due course, Garbo was despatched to Lisbon where he filed fake reports to the Germans, whilst pretending to be in London. The information he supplied to German intelligence was a judicious mixture of complete fiction, genuine information of insignificant military value, and genuine, valuable military intelligence artificially delayed in order to avoid danger to the Allies yet prove the veracity of Garbo's sources. The details of movements in Britain and descriptions of the British countryside he gained from reading a *Blue Guide to Britain*, French newspapers, a Portuguese book on the British naval fleet, a French-English dictionary of military terminology and a map of Britain given to him in Madrid. Unbelievably, Garbo spoke no English.[9] Staying at the Suisso Atlântico Hotel, a run-down hotel up a side street just off Restauradores next to a clanking tramline terminus, he had easy access to the Teatro da Rua dos Condes cinema newsreels (for propaganda news) and to the post office. From here he would send reports to the Nazis, using Portuguese postage stamps which he claimed were bought for him by a sympathetic British commercial pilot on the BOAC Bristol-Lisbon run. The imaginary pilot would then post the reports to Berlin. It was from his base in Lisbon that Garbo was able to send reports which made a significant contribution to deceiving the Nazis about the positioning of the D-Day invasions. Berlin was persuaded that the feared invasion would come in the Pas de Calais, a much shorter sea-crossing, rather than further west on the Normandy beaches. Garbo's deception was supported by the existence of airfields of fake planes, rows of inflatable tanks and of military trucks travelling about the area transmitting bogus radio chatter.

---

[9] Webster J. *The Spy with 29 Names*. London: Chatto & Windus.

The entire double agents system had been leading towards this moment – the successful invasion of continental Europe by massive numbers of Allied troops which could only bring about the final destruction of the German forces. And with the invasion of France came the almost immediate end of the wolfram trade.

Garbo's deception of the Germans was not discovered until after the war. On 29 July 1944 (just weeks after D-Day) he was awarded the Iron Cross by Germany for services to the Nazi cause; he was awarded the MBE for his service to the Allied cause just five months later.

Key locations in Lisbon

A key centre for spies and refugees in central Lisbon was the Pastelaria Suiça, a coffee shop, in Rossio Square. For Lisbon's men it was a welcome opportunity to see the legs of female refugees, unfettered as they were by the strict Portuguese dress code which still demanded that they be covered by long skirts. For Lisbon women, a favourite pastime was taking a pencil and a drawing pad along to the Suiça to sketch the new fashions emerging from elsewhere in Europe. Of course, not all refugees could afford sartorial elegance and some female refugees would use their alluring appearance to enhance their subsistence, not necessarily wearing their clothes in order to do so. Given that no refugee was permitted to work in the formal economy, for married women this illicit income was accepted by husbands and families as a necessary way of shortening their stay in Lisbon before finding freedom elsewhere in the world. For spies, of course, patronising the Suiça was a way of tracking movements and, in such a crowded venue, of keeping in touch with contacts.

Two other central Lisbon venues were also key centres for refugees and spies alike – the Teatro Politeama and the Teatro da Rua dos Condes. The Politeama was in the area of Lisbon equivalent to New York's Broadway. It was a theatre and entertainment district which attracted such international theatre stars who could still travel, like Leslie Howard (referred to in Chapter 4) and Josephine Baker. The latter was a black American-born French dancer who would later become a civil rights activist because of her experiences of racism. Each show was preceded by a half hour newsreel, edited to suit the prejudices of the audience that day. Baker, no longer able to perform freely in France, had been recruited by the French intelligence service and would conceal secret messages for the Allies in her bra. The Teatro da Rua dos Condes would become the Condes Cinema post-war but in the 1940s it showed newsreels and became a regular haunt of agent Garbo. Today, it retains the 1951 Estado Novo architectural exterior of the cinema, but houses the Hard Rock café.

Figure 21. The Condes Cinema, frequented by Agent Garbo taken from the Suisso Atlântico Hotel.

Just across the road from the Condes lies Lisbon's main railway station, Rossio, linking the city nationally and internationally. As such, it was an essential haunt for spies, who kept a close eye on all rail movements of goods and passengers. Even with today's modernised appearance, it takes little imagination to envisage the furtive observations, tailing and haranguing of passengers from the upstairs platforms. But it was not always so easy. Adjoining the station on the Avenida de Liberade side was the 5-star Avenida Palace Hotel, with its luxurious foyer and public rooms … and a wartime secret. The upstairs of the hotel had a secret door, leading directly onto Rossio's platforms, thus bypassing the ticket booths and main entrance on the station's lower level. The right word with hotel management would allow access to this secret entrance and exit whilst PVDE and enemy agents' attention was temporarily diverted elsewhere.

The British Council was a frequent venue of the literati and the movers and shakers in Lisbon. Its Lisbon base had evolved from the English Institute at Coimbra University, at that time the oldest and most prestigious university in the country. The Council's role was to interpret British life and thought to Portugal and, primarily through the teaching of English, to strengthen cultural relations between the two nations. It was certainly not overtly connected with espionage, although a *Glasgow Herald* headline in 1939 referred to the Council's work in 'Countering Totalitarian Penetration'. It undertook its mission through the teaching of English, a well-stocked library, lectures by visiting speakers from Britain, and publications (including medical and science bulletins), as well as a highly-respected programme of exhibitions, music, drama and films. From 1942, it occupied the newly-refurbished Palácio Menino de Ouro in Rua Luís Fernandes, close to the Botanical Gardens. The Council offered a welcome cultural experience in English for the many nationalities residing in wartime Lisbon. It attracted a wealth of high-profile speakers, artists and others, including cultural and military historians whose role fell little short of propaganda.[10] One photograph in the Council's archives shows such a lecture in full

---

[10] See Corse E. (2014). *A Battle For Neutral Europe: British Cultural Propaganda During the Second World War*. London: Bloomsbury.

swing, with uniformed members of the audience occupying the front row. Among them were PVDE and Abwehr agents, absorbing information to report back to their masters. "They are the easy ones to spot", a senior Council staff member told me. "Can you see the pale foreheads? That's because they usually wore their trilby hats pulled right down."

Figure 22. The British Council offices in Lisbon.

Secret intelligence battles

Of course, the principal aim of British intelligence was to thwart German intelligence – and vice versa. Given the possibility of shipping wolfram to Germany by sea, a close eye was kept on shipping movements along the Lisbon waterfront. On one occasion[11], a German

---

[11] As cited in Page M. (2002). *The First Global Village: How Portugal Changed the World*. (19th ed. 2014). Afragide: Casa das Letras. p239

ship was loaded with boxes of sand which replicated the appearance of wolfram cargo. Not long after sailing and before the deception was identified, the ship was blown up, creating the impression of a British victory. In fact, it was a decoy and no precious wolfram was actually lost. On another occasion, at a time of meagre rationing for many, Lisbon citizens were incensed to discover railway wagons stencilled "surplus food", allegedly a gift by the government of the generous Portuguese people to their German cousins. Civil disturbance broke out, with infuriated housewives claiming that this was an insult to their own patriotic efforts to feed their hungry families. In fact, the wagons contained wolfram, so the trick of suggesting that ordinary Portuguese citizens supported Germany had backfired. By contrast, an example of British intelligence deception also embraced a wider Portuguese public. Cargoes marked 'sardine tins' were loaded onto a ship.[12] The tins actually contained sand but the cargo successfully caused the further outrage that British agents fully intended among the populace.

Some British secret intelligence service agents were to become well-known in future years. There were other agents besides Ian Fleming within the Iberian department of MI6, which was based in Madrid. During the early part of the war it had no Portuguese section, so the Department Head, Kim Philby (himself to become a Soviet agent later), used the offices of the Shell Oil Company in Lisbon as cover for the Special Operations Executive (SOE). Philby set up his friend Graham Greene as the Portuguese section head, as Greene had been recently dismissed from his West African post. Here he had been attempting unsuccessfully to persuade his boss to set up a mobile brothel to run the length of the West African coast, seducing German naval and U-boat officers on shore leave who would then unburden themselves of their secret movements. Greene was to use his experiences in West Africa later in several of his novels, such as *A Burnt-Out Case* and *Heart of the Matter*. Greene also wrote the screenplay for the espionage film *The Third Man*, which is regarded as a cinematic masterpiece. It is well-documented that he used Philby as a model for one of the characters, the unscrupulous Harry Lime. One of Philby's agents, with specific responsibility for safeguarding Allied shipping off the African coast

[12] Further cited in Page, op. cit. p239

Chapter 5

was a young Malcolm Muggeridge, who later became a renowned journalist, broadcaster and stimulator of theological debate.

Famous though these latter participants were to become, the activity of wolfram's extraction was undertaken by hundreds of anonymous workers in the mountainous Beira district, as we shall see in Chapter 7.

Chapter 6
Wolfram by Day and
Fornication by Night

The pursuit of wolfram became an all-absorbing activity for government officials, as well as the businesses and miners directly involved in its extraction. There was involvement at all levels from Portuguese ministers, to diplomats and governments of both Germany and the Allied powers. Salazar is reputed to have observed that nothing caused him so much loss of sleep as the wolfram question, given that "the desire for neutrality cannot be superior to the interests of the nation."[1]

British Embassy official David Eccles wrote to his wife back in London about the frantic exchange of messages between the US Embassies in Lisbon and Washington regarding the commodity. In December 1941, a Portuguese merchant ship, the *Corte Real*, was attacked and sunk by a U-boat while on its way to the USA with, as Germany was to claim later, a cargo of the ore. Eccles wrote to his wife from Lisbon that the "wolfram business goes from bad to worse, the Germans have now sunk a Portuguese ship carrying wolfram to the USA to warn this wretched little country that they mean to stop at nothing to secure wolfram for themselves and to deny it to us and America". Indeed, Eccles was to add to the letter, later, that "we find it untrue that the ship had any wolfram."[2]

Eccles played a vital role in monitoring this trade, acting as a go-between of the Portuguese government and suppliers. With a background in business, he had joined the British Ministry of Economic Warfare and been drafted to Lisbon in April 1940. Here he set up new offices and found that the British Ambassador, Walford Selby,

---

[1] Radio address to nation in 1942

[2] Ibid. p309

Chapter 6

entrusted him to liaise directly with the government. Astute and experienced businessman though he was, Eccles observed that the freedom to deal with Salazar directly, whilst an honour which he enjoyed, had its downsides. Though he considered that he and Salazar had a good rapport, conducting their conversations in French, the diplomat thought that he must never be caught out and that preparing for meetings with the Prime Minister was akin to being grilled in his student tutorial days at Oxford.[3]

His descriptions of the Lisbon he had initially found were idyllic. In letters to his wife, he praised the abundance of flowers, the scents, the "best orange juice in the world" and the finery surrounding the diplomatic lifestyle. The countryside was magnificent and yet restful. But such descriptions belied both the delicacy in handling such a "complex and gifted" man as Salazar and the complicated economic situation – "the harbour reflects the blue of heaven, there go half a hundred ships, with or without navicerts…who cares". Furthermore, he observed that the atmosphere of the British Embassy was full of scandals and flirtations and liaisons between staff. His wife's response was:

> *"Your stories are good. Wolfram by day and fornication by night – your colleagues must eclipse in gallantry all other competitors in Dr Salazar's raffish capital."*[4]

So strong was the professional rapport with Eccles that Salazar would seek the advice of the British diplomat on many aspects of Anglo-Portuguese relations. Returning to London for a new post with the Ministry in late 1941, Eccles found himself despatched again to Lisbon in the new year of 1942 because relations with Salazar had turned sour. London believed that Eccles was the person to soothe the way to harmonious relations.

---

[3] Weber R. (2011). *The Lisbon Route: Entry and Escape in Nazi Europe*. Ivan R Dee: Plymouth. p279

[4] Eccles, D. (1983). *By Safe Hand: Letters of Sybil and David Eccles, 1939-1942*. Bodley Head: London.

The supplies of wolfram, as we saw in Chapter 5, were closely-monitored. For example, Salazar would not supply Italy with it on the grounds that Mussolini (whose photograph he reportedly had on his desk) might divert it to Germany and thus upset the delicate balance of equal treatment of both sets of belligerents. For wolfram to reach Italy, it would need to travel south from Portugal and through the Straits of Gibraltar into the Mediterranean. This area was of crucial significance to our next government agent.

Ian Fleming

It was the Straits of Gibraltar, from the Atlantic to the Mediterranean, which became the responsibility of another Briton, naval Commander Ian Fleming. In reality, Fleming's career after his Eton College education did not go as planned. He failed in his effort to join the Foreign Office, joining instead the Reuters News Agency in 1931. Nevertheless, from an early stage in the war, Fleming had been selected by the Director of Naval Intelligence to occupy a key role and he became privy to a range of covert operations. What was apparent to the Navy was here was a man who was a cool-headed strategist, a thinker, and a plotter. "Clear thought and rapid response were the tools of his trade."[5] This made him ideal to head up so-called Operation Goldeneye, the plan to monitor Franco's Spain and its potential alliance with the Nazis.

As noted in Chapter 3, Salazar was very anxious about the status of Spain which, if brought into the war on the Axis side, could spell the end of Portugal's independence and neutrality. Operation Goldeneye also covered plans to protect Gibraltar from possible invasion by the Nazis, an action which would have a catastrophic impact on shipping in and out of the Mediterranean. In February 1941, Fleming flew out to Gibraltar to monitor shipping through the Straits and Mediterranean military installations.

Hand in hand with Operation Goldeneye, was the parallel Operation Tracer, for which Fleming also had responsibility. If the Nazis were to

---

[5] According to Cabel C. (2008). *Ian Fleming's Secret War*. Barnsley: Pen & Sword. p3.

Chapter 6

invade and capture Gibraltar, this operation entailed sealing six military volunteers within the eponymous Rock to monitor, from within a cavern, enemy movements through two small slits. Contact with British forces would be maintained via radio contact, operated by a bicycle-operated generator. Estimates vary on the amount of food and water to be supplied to the volunteers – between one and seven years' worth. Volunteers were recruited, including an officer, two doctors and three wireless operators. It was made clear to volunteers that, once sealed in the Rock, there was no way out. If they died, they would be embalmed and cemented into the cavern wall.

Of course, Goldeneye was never operationalised and plans were only scaled back when the threat of Nazi invasion or collaboration between Franco and Germany was reduced in May 1943 after the capture of North Africa and the subsequent driving out of the Axis powers from Sicily the following August.

Like many other intelligence officers, Fleming made frequent sorties to where he was needed, including to Portugal. From here he could monitor activity across the Iberian peninsula. As with other British agents, the favoured base was the Palácio Hotel in Estoril, referred to in Chapter 4. Just downriver from Lisbon, Estoril lay in sharp contrast to the sometimes dusty and hot capital. Its elegant gardens, luxury hotels, and views over the idyllic, azure estuary belied the espionage activity beneath.

As new arrivals checked in to the Palácio, they were met with attentive care – overtly by the hotel staff and covertly by British, American or Gestapo secret service agents. Whether innocent holidaymakers (travelling to one of the last free resorts in Europe) or regal, military, diplomatic or business guests (particularly wolfram agents), many knew what was going on.

For Fleming, it was his office base and he was there on a specific mission in May 1941. On his way from London to Washington, he stopped off in Lisbon and Estoril to monitor the activities of Dusko Popov (see Chapter 5). At the adjoining casino, Fleming played the tables and witnessed an event where Popov placed a bet of $40,000 ($643,529 at 2016 values), causing a rival to withdraw from the baccarat table. This incident made a powerful impression on Fleming who commented to a colleague:

"What if those men had been German secret service agents, and suppose that we had cleaned them out of their money; now that would have been exciting."[6]

Certainly, it was a sufficiently memorable episode for Fleming to later use the scene in his first novel, *Casino Royale*, although the casino featured here was in Royale-les-Eaux, France. The description is not always glamorous:

"The scent and smoke and sweat of a casino are nauseating at three in the morning. Then the soul erosion produced by high gambling – a compost of greed and fear and nervous tension – becomes unbearable, the senses awake and revolt from it."[7]

In the 1969 Bond film *On Her Majesty's Secret Service*, the pre-credit hotel and coastal shots feature the Palácio Hotel, the sea-front, and the nearby Guincho coast just north of the estuary mouth.

The links with Fleming and Bond do not stop there. Fleming masterminded Operation Goldeneye, and its name was used as the title of the 1995 Bond film (although it was not written by Fleming). He also called his house in Jamaica, where he wrote all his Bond novels, by the same name. In 1956, Fleming played host for a month to the serving British Prime Minister Sir Anthony Eden. During the Second World War, Eden had proved himself the key Iberian specialist, a close adviser of Churchill and he strove hard to maintain the support of Salazar. Eden's health had collapsed after the Suez Crisis, the first major conflict in which Britain had been involved since the war. Passing at one stage after Fleming's death to singer Bob Marley, the estate is now called the Goldeneye Hotel and Resort which, like the Palácio in Estoril, is a luxury, boutique hotel.

Endowed with public-school charm, quick-wittedness and an ability to think laterally, Fleming also had a reputation for aloofness. These are all pre-requisites of a spy perhaps, but it is easy to forget that, besides

---

[6] Online blog by Prof. Neill Lochery: *The Real-life Rick's Café*. 13 October, 2014. http://www.neill-lochery.co.uk/blog/the-real-life-rick-s-caf-_1.html

[7] Opening lines of: Fleming I. (1953) *Casino Royale*. London: Jonathan Cape.

creating the fictional character of James Bond, Fleming was also the creator of the 1964 children's book *Chitty Chitty Bang Bang: The Musical Car*.

It has frequently been mooted that Popov was the real-life inspiration of the James Bond character – a debonair, fast-living, womaniser with a love of powerful cars. Certainly, Popov was one of around ten people who made a considerable impact upon Fleming. Just how much of an impact is speculation.

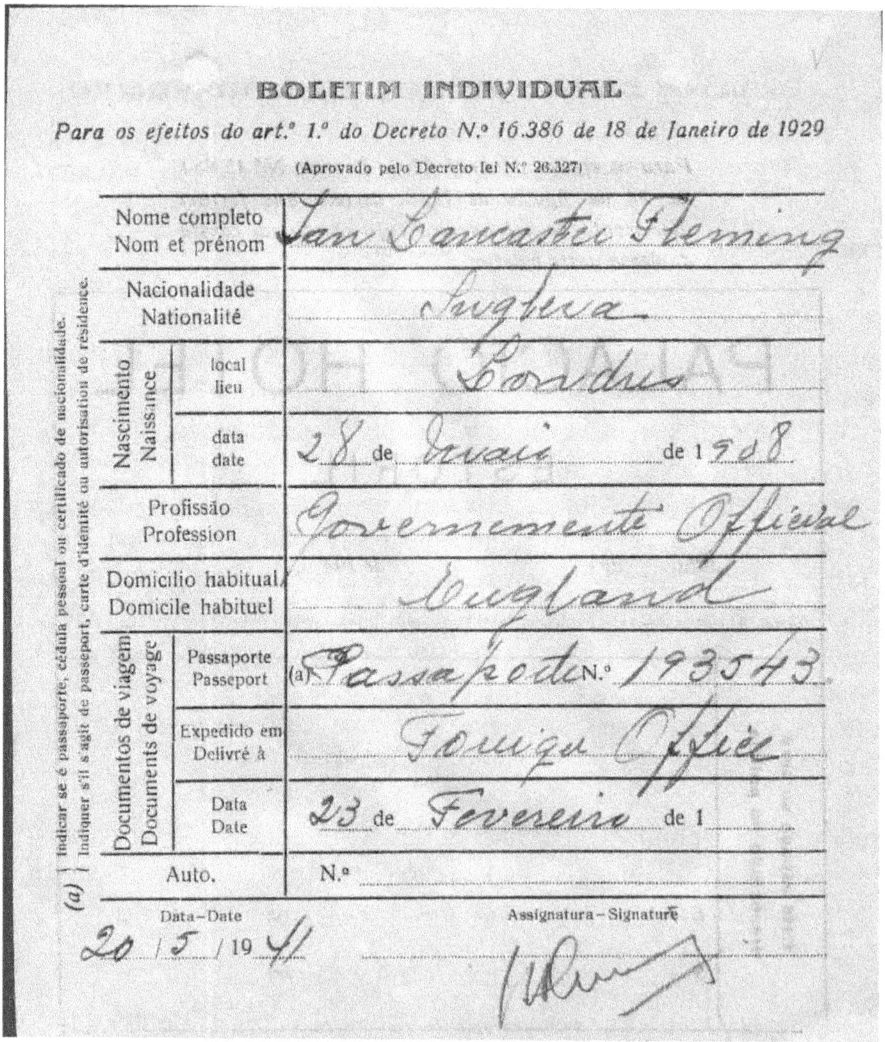

BOLETIM INDIVIDUAL

Para os efeitos do art.º 1.º do Decreto N.º 16.386 de 18 de Janeiro de 1929

(Aprovado pelo Decreto lei N.º 26.327)

Nome completo / Nom et prénom		Ian Lancaster Fleming
Nacionalidade / Nationalité		Inglesa
Nascimento / Naissance	local / lieu	Londres
	data / date	28 de Maio de 1908
Profissão / Profession		Government Official
Domicilio habitual / Domicile habituel		England
Documentos de viagem / Documents de voyage	Passaporte / Passeport	(a) Passaporte N.º 193543
	Expedido em / Delivré à	Foreign Office
	Data / Date	23 de Fevereiro de 1
Auto.		N.º

(a) Indicar se é passaporte, cédula pessoal ou certificado de nacionalidade. / Indiquer s'il s'agit de passeport, carte d'identité ou autorisation de résidence.

Data–Date: 20 / 5 / 1941

Assignatura – Signature

Figure 23. Registration form for Ian Fleming at the Palácio Hotel.

Treasure

Not all spies have the good looks of the fictional Bond, nor are all spies men. Lily Sergeyev occupies one of the strangest roles of wartime agents in Lisbon, and her MI5 codename, Agent Treasure, was surely one of the least apt names devised. Her volatile personality and activities would cause great anxiety to the Head of the Double-Cross Committee, Tar Robertson (see Chapter 5) and others.

Born Nathalie Sergueiew in St Petersburg in 1912, her family fled to Paris at the outbreak of the Russian Revolution. Training as a journalist, she became fluent in English, French and German, as well as her native Russian. Her early journalistic career in the 1930s saw her interview Hermann Goering and, after the fall of France, she agreed to become an Abwehr agent (for whom she was given the codename Tramp). Travelling to Spain with her doted-on dog, Babs, she introduced herself also to MI5 and was appointed a double-agent for the British. However, her appointment came with a condition – one laid down by her (not by MI5). This was that, in due course, she could take the terrier-poodle Babs back to Britain. Therein lay the problem and one which almost led to catastrophe.

Britain had strict quarantine laws and to abide by these, Babs needed to be quarantined in the safe-haven of Gibraltar before return to London. Treasure reluctantly agreed and Babs was despatched. Alas, in Gibraltar, Babs was run over and killed in a motoring accident and the devastating impact of this on Treasure was to have significant ramifications for her time in Lisbon.

Her cover story was that, like film-maker Alfred Hitchcock, she was gathering intelligence for the Ministry of Information for propaganda films. Lily's Gestapo handler, Major Emil Kleimann, had a soft spot for her. To maximise the beneficial impact of this, prior to her next trip to Lisbon, Lily bought a gift for him in Dunhill's in London's Piccadilly – an engraved pigskin wallet. Landing in Lisbon on 1 March 1944, Lily headed for the usual rendezvous, the Palácio Hotel, only to find that Kleimann not yet arrived. A young, blond agent, Koppe, came to her hotel room to advise of his boss's delay, indicating that he would arrive 'soon'.

Chapter 6

Like David Eccles several years earlier, Lily was entranced by the spring blossom and scent of Estoril, particularly after the misery of gloomy London. Yet that was no solace in her long wait, day after day, for Kleimann, whom British secret sources indicated was now under threat of the sack for his inefficiency – compared with Berlin's pleasure with her own work. Fourteen days later, she was taken to meet the Gestapo agent in central Lisbon, and he appeared with great drama from behind the playful fountains in the Place Pombal. Speaking ecstatically about seeing her again and how her own work had helped him, he shepherded her to an empty apartment, in which he displayed his own gift to her – a wireless transmitter disguised inside a shabby case. He would arrange for a wireless specialist to show her how to use Morse code. But first, off to Sintra for lunch.

Travelling up to the nearby fort in Sintra, Kleimann had praised Lily for her work in telling Berlin about bomb damage in Britain. To celebrate the occasion and succumbing to her cover story, he took several shots – on Lily's small Zeiss camera – of himself, herself and of them together. Lily could not believe his stupidity in making a public record of his appearance with her. Over lunch she presented him with the Dunhill wallet, a small object that she had easily transported to Lisbon; he handed her a bracelet and £300 in notes plus 20,000 escudos for her troubles. More money, he promised, would follow tomorrow.

The conversation turned serious, with muted but detailed discussion about invasion plans. Berlin needed to know where the invasions would take place, and what preparations were going on at Bristol docks with transport arriving from America. Lily (or Tramp as her Abwehr codename was) should use the transmitter three times a week to send brief messages for fear of interception. Kleimann passed to her a single British postal stamp with microdot in the top-left corner. This contained instructions for using the transmitter in case she forgot.

The next morning she was trained by Koppe in Morse Code. Kleimann arrived with more money (£1500 in single notes in a paper bag!). Explaining that she would send the case containing the transmitter via the diplomatic bag, the Gestapo minder asked no questions about the apparent safety of this means of transport.

Exchanges over, a key issue remained. Lily needed to identify a 'control signal' to indicate that she was now transmitting under British control. Kleimann made a suggestion which she immediately rejected. Instead, she proposed adding a dash between the message and the number. Given that any message would be repeated, sometimes a dash would be there, sometimes not. But … if the dash appeared *twice* – once in the message, once in the repetition, it would mean that she was no longer free.

How could such a technique prove so fraught? In her diary, she wrote:

> *"Five months ago I was so full of enthusiasm, so ready to love the British, so eager to help them. I admired them; I trusted them; I had faith in British fair play. I worked readily for them; I took risks on their behalf. In return I only asked for one thing: to keep my dog. It wasn't asking much, but it was too much for them! Tomorrow I'll be in London, I'll hand them over the money, the code, the radio, everything … except for a dash! A dash that will enable me to destroy all my work, all their work, the minute I want to. I shall not use my power. But I will know that I have them at my mercy!"*[8]

As D-Day approached, Treasure's fury was such that she openly informed MI5 of the secret signal. When he learned of this, Tar Robinson was incensed. Treasure now had the means, if she chose, to bring down her whole double-agent work with a double dash. And the reason for this? Because she was so distraught about the loss of her dog, Babs, and was laying the blame for this squarely at the feet of the British.

Treasure continued to undertake valued work for the British on the preparations for D-Day. But she had lost the confidence of MI5 and was advised a week after D-Day that her services were no longer required. However, messages continued to be sent from her code-name for several months in order to further deceive the Germans. As for Lily, she moved to the United States, bitter about her experience, calling MI5 "gangsters", before dying at just 38 years old in 1950, with her memoirs being published posthumously.

---

[8] Sergueiev L. (1968). *Secret Service Rendered: An Agent in the Espionage Duel Preceding the Invasion of France*. London: William Kimber.

Chapter 6

Ecclesiastic

If Treasure was considered volatile in character yet plain in appearance, another double-agent gained attention for her looks as well as her abilities, a glamorous twenty-two year old woman code named Ecclesiastic. The mistress of Abwehr officer Franz Koschnik, this central European woman had previously worked for the Polish secret service, targeting Italian diplomats. Taken on by SIS, the forerunner of MI6, she became based in Lisbon and she used the Abwehr relationship to pass on false information, including misleading claims over the damage German bombs were inflicting on London.

In particular, her brief was to focus on the V-1 rockets. The Germans were told that Piccadilly Circus and Leicester Square had been totally destroyed. This was not implausible: when Churchill showed his War Cabinet in February 1943 aerial photographs taken by the RAF of the rocket-launch installations around Calais, it was confirmation of the threat they most dreaded.[9] As we saw in Chapter 2, it was well-known that no substance other than wolfram could withstand the enormous heat and pressure of the heat in the jet nozzles. The intention of the misinformation was to leave the enemy unsure about how successful the targeting of their V rockets was proving, so as to misdirect future attacks.

Ecclesiastic was handled by MI6 officer Klop Ustinov (codename U35), father of the actor, writer and raconteur Peter Ustinov. Klop became paranoid about aspects of his work, particularly because of the dubious characters with whom he was forced to mingle. He was concerned about the relationship with the head of the Portuguese police whom he knew was taking bribes from the Germans. Warned that his life was at risk, he always stood at the rear of a lift to avoid being stabbed in the back by a poisoned hypodermic needle, was concerned that his food might be poisoned, or that he might be trapped in a liaison with an enemy female agent. Nevertheless, Klop was entranced by Ecclesiastic, writing that she clearly enjoyed "the game of mobilizing her ample female resources against normal male instincts". At the same

---

[9] Page M. (2002). *The First Global Village – How Portugal Changed The World.* Alfragide: Casa das Letras. p236

time, he bemoaned (possibly with an air of jealousy?) her relationship with Koschnik:

> "*I have made clear to her that to live with the Abwehr is not quite helpful enough and that more concrete results must be achieved before her activities for us can be termed a success.*"[10]

In fact, Ecclesiastic was to prove extremely successful through to the end of the war and holds the unique position of being the only double-agent to be photographed at work. An image of her photographing British documents in Lisbon in 1944 was taken by Koschnik, presumably as insurance over her. He gave her a copy which survives only because she passed it on immediately to her MI6 handler.[11]

Fritz Cramer and Otto John

Fritz Cramer was a man in Klop Ustinov's sights. Formerly the secretary of the upmarket Hotel Adlon in Berlin, Cramer's Lisbon home was the similarly luxurious Hotel Atlântico in Estoril, where he lived the high life, had a mistress and was in frequent contact with Klop. The latter had been despatched to Lisbon by Kim Philby, head of the Iberian section of MI6, to conduct psychological warfare, where his role included spreading concern and fear among the local SS about the potential war crimes with which they would be charged when peace came. In fact, both Cramer and fellow agent Otto John had anti-Nazi sympathies which were to become further entwined later in the war. John had been the chief lawyer for the Lufthansa airline and arrived in Lisbon in this role in November 1942. Here he approached MI6 to indicate that there was a strong anti-Nazi movement in Berlin. Returning to Lisbon in early 1943, he updated MI6 on the movement's progress and in May 1943 was involved in an assassination attempt on Hitler's life. MI6 responded coolly, not wishing to raise any Soviet suspicions about an anti-Nazi movement in Germany. When a further attempt also failed in 1944, John fled to Madrid, where he contacted

---

[10] Quoted in: Jeffrey K. (2010). *MI6: The History of the Secret Intelligence Service 1909-1949*. London: Bloomsbury.

[11] The image can be seen at http://www.bbc.co.uk/news/uk-11379259 : *MI6 secrets revealed in first official history* (referring to the Jeffrey book immediately above).

Chapter 6

MI6 and was sent to a safe house in Lisbon. Here the PVDE conducted a raid, mistakenly believing that John was an RAF pilot. They tipped off the Abwehr, and Cramer was commanded to personally assassinate John. Instead, he alerted MI6 who negotiated John's safe release into British hands; this action apparently saving Cramer from trial post-war.

Lunch with strangers

Misrepresentation of information is a key aspect of espionage and no agent had a clearer task in this respect than David Walker. Like Klop, his focus was psychological warfare – specifically through the creation of 'sibs' (short for sibilant, a hissing sound, a whisper in the ear). His role was similar to Chinese whispers – mumbled comments which get out of control and blown out of proportion.

Formerly a journalist with the *Daily Mirror*, Walker was despatched to Lisbon from London by the covert espionage and subversion group, the Special Operations Executive (SOE). Here his cover was to be a staff correspondent of the *Mirror* (which was true). As an agent, he deployed various deception techniques and mixed freely with German journalists and agents in the capital's many bars, nightclubs and cafes. Weekly he met an attractive woman in one of the central coffee houses. They talked, gossiped, and attracted attention. When she left, Walker would stay to pay the bill and would pick up the newspaper left by the woman. Inside were a series of handwritten, apparently random words from her, just the sort of thing a journalist or crossword puzzle devotee might do. These were the initial ideas from which Walker would create his 'sibs' to destroy enemy morale.

His sibs had an element of truth about them – something which could become intentionally distorted. For example, the conditions faced by German soldiers in the march on Russia in 1941. Walker would help spread accounts of the extent of frostbite, amputations, and related distressing illnesses affecting soldiers in order to demoralise German citizens. Likewise, economic targets included the huge German conglomerate I G Farben[12] which included companies such as the

---

[12] I G Farben was broken up post-war into its constituent parts, e.g. Agfa-Gevaert, Bayer, BASF, Hoescht, etc. This was partly to dissociate the company from its manufacture of Zyklon-B, the gas used in the holocaust death camps. When the

Bayer chemical company, inventors of aspirin. Walker set about the myth that taking aspirin could lead to impotence and that rival headache cures did not have the same impact.

Walker was ambivalent about the impact that his efforts had in terms of propaganda.[13] He took on the role of correspondent for other newspapers, including the London *Times* when their correspondent was expelled, married a Portuguese citizen, and lived as if he was merely a happy resident of the country. In the summer of 1944, with the agreement of SOE who considered that the war was in its closing stages, he replaced a *Daily Mirror* correspondent killed on D-Day, and during the final months of the war in Europe, he became correspondent covering the American Ninth Army's push through Holland into Germany.

As this chapter illustrates, a varied and colourful group of spies thrived in this small city for the duration of the hostilities. Their work underpinned the espionage carried on in connection with wolfram and other goods and people in transit through Portugal.

Holocaust Memorial was being constructed in Berlin in 2003, there was outrage that two of the supplying companies, Bayer and Degussa, were successor companies to IG Farben and had made products for the death camps. Other bodies, including the German Protestant Church, argued strongly that involving the companies was a symbol of forgiveness and reconciliation.

[13] Walker D E. (1957) *Lunch with a Stranger*. London: Allan Wingate.

Chapter 7
Wolfram Rush

No product, process or factor was to be more important in Salazar's exercise of maintaining neutrality than the pursuit of wolfram. By 1942, Portugal had become the main European producer of the ore, with Spain and Sweden in second and third places respectively. Wolfram was considered to be vital to the war efforts and Germany committed to buy as much as it possibly could, particularly from 1941 when demand exploded.

In keeping with his principles, Salazar provided both sets of belligerents with wolfram, reflecting his 'right to choose' policy for the nation to do with as it wished for its own resources. It also aligned with the spirit of the Anglo-Portuguese Treaty and avoided any temptation by Germany to simply invade the country and plunder whatever it wanted. As the struggle for the Portuguese supplies began, Britain's Ministry of Economic Warfare began to implement programmes to deny wolfram to Germany, a position assisted by the entry of the USA into the conflict from 1941.

Britain had a number of advantages[1] regarding supplies of the ore: the support of the USA; the British ownership of the most prolific and important mining company in the Beira Alta region (the Beralt Tin and Wolfram Company at Panasqueira); the greater number of personnel in the country with longer experience of mining, refining and export; and near-monopoly ownership of telephone and telegraphic communication in the nation. By contrast, the German-controlled interests were smaller and less important, although Germany had invested significantly in other infrastructure and heavy industry facilities in Portugal. Post-war, files were released from the secret services corroborating the extensive efforts made by German companies to embed themselves not just in

---

[1] Wheeler D L. (1986). The Price of Neutrality: Portugal, the Wolfram Question and World War II. *Luso-Brazilian Review*, Vol 23. No 1. pp 107-127.

Chapter 7

mining companies but also many other significant aspects of Portuguese life, in order to influence policy, or at least to keep an ear close to the ground about developments.[2]

However, whilst Britain's greatest advantage was the financial arrangement with Portugal whereby the latter became a debtor nation to the UK, conversely this gave Germany another advantage. In return for being willing (indeed, desperate) to buy as much wolfram as possible, Germany was reducing Portugal's dependency on Britain through money-laundering arrangements, particularly through the Banco Espírito Santo.

The wolfram war fell into three phases: firstly, the free market, from the outbreak of war in September 1939 through to February 1942. During this time, Germany increased its presence in Portugal, setting up officials, agents and technicians attached to its formal Legation. German finance secured German-owned mines or made enticing offers to Portuguese companies which mined wolfram.

The second phase was marked by the establishment in March 1942 of the United Kingdom Commercial Corporation (UKCC) to deny German pre-emptive purchases[3] of wolfram. This work was reinforced by its US counterpart, the United States Commercial Company, which even shared the same offices in Lisbon and Madrid.

The third phase was under the auspices of the newly-created Portuguese Metals Commission which became operative from summer 1942. Under this arrangement there were two distinct categories of wolfram: 'recognised' ore from registered, official mines (whether owned by Portuguese, Allied or German companies), and 'free' ore from independent operators. Overall, the principal production and export period was from the middle of 1941 through to August 1944.

---

[2] Declassified information from US files.

[3] The aim of this was strategy was to buy up supplies simply so that your enemy could not gain them.

The mines

Given the informality and subterfuge surrounding so much of this work, it is difficult to ascertain accurate numbers of people involved in wolfram-related employment. They are estimated[4] at 80-90,000 but these figures exclude non-mining jobs in supply and transportation aspects, and of clerical tasks undertaken in Lisbon, Oporto, and elsewhere. The total must surely have nudged 100,000 in total.

Mineral mining in northern Portugal had been established in Roman times, as recorded by the Roman writer, Pliny the Elder, who was Governor of Iberia from AD 70-75.[5] His observations on mining techniques would not have been too far out of place right up until the nineteenth century. But from the turn of the twentieth century, the big mining companies were either British or German-owned. The largest mine, Panasqueira, was in the hands of the British, whilst German companies owned two mid-size concerns and several smaller ones. The second largest, Borralha, further north than others, belonged to Vichy Government concerns (in Occupied France), supported by German capital. Productivity required outside investment beyond the means of the local population and ore prices reflected the peaks and troughs of activity. So, for the most part, the mining villages remained undeveloped – economically, socially and educationally. Families stayed put, battling poverty and disease and without the financial wherewithal or the aspiration to move elsewhere. With their limited knowledge and experience, would not the locals have imagined that all of Portugal, or the world, was like this – harsh and unforgiving? Working here meant hard graft, doing the bidding of the owners and putting up with grim conditions.

Differences between mines

The mining areas around the Beira are high in the mountains, suffering harsh winters alternating with hot, dusty summers. The terrain is steep

---

[4] Wheeler, op.cit. p113-114

[5] See Page, M. (2002). *The First Global Village – How Portugal Changed The World*. Alfragide: Casa das Letras. pp43-45

Chapter 7

and not easy to farm: much of it is too high to grow olives, with pockets of land too small to make oak cork viable, too steep for many crops, and too barren for cattle. The age-old farming communities existed on pine forestry, rearing sheep, and mining minerals. Some mines, with significant investment, grew to be large concerns; others remained small works established in hillsides, rather like the old, small drift mines which are still evident in some parts of the UK.

By far the largest producer (at 125 hectares of surface land) was Panasqueira. Established late in the nineteenth century, it was renamed the Wolfram Mining and Smelting Company in 1911. Production boomed during the war years before it was closed in 1944. A whole village of workers' dwellings was built into the hillside, almost replicating the layout of some South Wales mining valleys – serried ranks of dwellings zig-zagging down the hillside – although here with terracotta roof tiles rather than Welsh slate. Another British-owned mine was at Regoufe, a mere five kilometres from the Mining Company of Northern Portugal's German-operated mine at Rio De Frades. Part of the road that led to the two sites was used by both parties and they agreed to share the cost of its upkeep!

Figure 24. The Panasqueira mine set high in the Beira Mountains.

Other German-owned operations (or those which supplied wolfram to Germany) included The Mine of Shadows, at the source of the River Vilamea, which became one of the greatest sources of wealth in the locality; Casaio (which was previously owned by a Belgian company later commandeered by the Nazis); Chas; Vale de Gatas; and Carris.

The outbreak of hostilities saw a sudden increase in activity from under 600 tons in 1937 to nearly 7,000 tons in 1943, with the result that shifts became longer and more regular, and new overseers moved into the area to ensure that targets were met. Agents appeared, driving cars up the rough tracks through the granite slabs rather than arriving by sure-footed mule or donkey. The workers could see that demand for wolfram was there. They were not concerned with why Britain and Germany were at war, but they knew that their leader (who told them that he knew what was best for them) had kept their country out of the conflict – at least this would not decimate the male population of the villages.

Even with this huge increase in production, the big companies could not supply all the demand. However, there were large numbers of small, independent mines which, as the price of wolfram soared, now became cost-effective to operate. These independent, unregulated operators, many with local knowledge, became known as 'fossickers'. They extracted ore from areas which the big companies had deemed unprofitable to work – either because the estimated reserves were too small or because the prevailing market value of wolfram had not made it profitable to extract from these workings. Now, as market values soared, it became worthwhile for wolfram fossickers (known locally as 'volframistas') to work the seams, risking their lives for the unheard of riches they could amass.

The atmosphere of the wolfram-rush

As in any 'gold rush'-like conditions, outsiders were attracted to the area, driven by a mixture of lust for promised wealth and by the poor conditions of their own home area. It was man's work – incoming families were not encouraged. Generally, there was no additional infrastructure of healthcare, schools or other facilities. The work was hard, involving long hours in bleak conditions and if you fell ill or had an accident, that was tough. You couldn't expect help or any social security safety net. But if you kept strong and healthy, there was a fortune to be made and you could send the profits home to your family. If you were local and your family was already here, there was little to spend the money on and certainly no savings culture for when the good times passed. Like the nineteenth century Californian and Yukon gold rushes or the Colorado silver rush[6], a macho culture grew up. Money was spent on wine, women and song – and the rest would be frittered away. Stories abounded of volframistas lighting celebratory cigars with rolled escudo notes; of sporting fine fountain pens from their jacket pockets or ordering books by the metre to fill newly-installed bookshelves even though they were illiterate; of high quality gold and jewelled wristwatches glistening on their wrists, even if few could tell the time.

> *"In Codeçais there was this guy, Bernardino, who had some land with a lot of ore and he smoked cigarettes made from banknotes because there wasn't any paper ... many made it good from ore, they knew how to take advantage."*[7]

Those working in the mines could make 18-20 escudos a day, substantially above a peasant's wage. As in gold mines, the men were searched[8] at the end of each shift to ensure that they were taking no contraband wolfram home, such was its increasing value. As prices rose, and the temptation to become an independent fossicker increased, people heard that they could get two hundred escudos for a small rock

---

[6] For a description of the Colorado silver rush mining towns see: Ashley R. On The Rocky Road to Ridgway. *Good Motoring*. Summer 2014. p28-31

[7] Oral history of local villager. Quoted in Lage. (2011). *The Significance Of The Tua Valley In The Context Of The Portuguese Wolfram Boom (1ˢᵗ Half Of The XX Century)*. In McCants, A (ed) et al. *Railroads in Historical Context: construction, costs and consequences*. FOTZUA; Vila Nova de Gaia: MIT (Portugal), EDP, University of Minho, 2011. Vol 1, p15-43. (Proceedings of the 1ˢᵗ International Conference of the International and Transdisciplinary Project FozTua, 2011).

[8] An excellent video (in Portuguese) of Nazi wolfram mining is available on YouTube® at: https://www.youtube.com/watch?v=o513tQ1lfzo. This includes the searching of miners at the end of their shift.

(fifty times their regular peasant wage) on the open market. Such was the temptation, the greed and the deception, that some prospectors were even known to fry quartz in lard until it became black and shiny. Then they would bury it somewhere where no other traces existed, just to mislead and confuse rival fossickers.

With little else to do in their spare time, men frequented the local bars where sales of brandy rose steeply. Rarely was their income spent wisely or invested.

Transporting the ore

Sometimes, even licensed ore was smuggled from the production areas to the buyers directly or via intermediaries. Such activity could be accomplished through a variety of ingenious means: from loading it on the back of wretched donkeys or mules who could traverse the woods and sinuous back paths across the Spanish border, to disguising it within other products transported by road or rail. Often it was shipped by rail to Lisbon or Oporto and onward by sea, or inland by rail across the border. All Iberian rail traffic to and from the French-Spanish border was supervised by the German Reich from a base in Barcelona. Its Lisbon agent was responsible for rail traffic to France, Switzerland, Sweden and Finland. Whilst records were kept of shipments, many of these became falsified as the war progressed and the demand for wolfram increased. Such deceit could occur in the mining compounds, on the railways or elsewhere, given that demand was seemingly unstoppable. Many goods in transit were camouflaged, whether on rail wagons or in trucks, adding to the danger of the trade and thus the potential profits to be made.

In addition to the Iberian-gauge railways there were some small, metric narrow-gauge tracks built specifically to haul ore to Oporto. Like the North Wales narrow-gauge steam railways designed to haul slate from the mountains to the sea-port of Porthmadog for export, these lines wove around the mountainous region of northern Portugal. They not only provided direct transit of ore but generated a side industry for smugglers, particularly on the Tua line heading to Oporto.

> *"At Brunheda station they drilled a trench and a lot of ore spilled out .... There was a vein that passed beneath the line.*

> *They let the train pass through ... and they were in the trench*
> *taking the ore. They would load the bags onto donkeys and*
> *would carry it away through whatever trails were possible.*
> *There were a lot of people involved and many who would buy.*
> *During those years of ore, nothing [agricultural] was produced.*
> *They would only mine, buy and sell the ore."*[9]

Sometimes the existence of a mine, geologically proven to extract a
different ore, was used as a front for falsifying production figures. The
police fought a losing battle to keep the records straight and to prevent
smuggling. In Lousa, for example, the Mining Group of Arouca was
fined 4,000 escudos in October 1941 for having received in their
washing plant a consignment of wolfram ore without documentation.
The ore had been purchased without the necessary paperwork and sold
on to trader António Pinho Moreira. In total, 470 kg of partly-processed
wolfram was confiscated in the area.[10]

Mining conditions

Conditions in the mines and their villages varied. In the small ones,
work was often still done by manually hewing out the mineral.
Dynamite was used in the larger ones, there was electrification of
lighting and jackhammers, underground rails led to the galleries and
there were washeries to separate mineral from rock. As local residents
at Moimenta[11] recalled:

> *"It was all drilled with air-hammers ... then the fire was*
> *prepared and the burst was made."* Antonio Mendes Pinto.

---

[9] Oral history of local villager. Quoted in Lage. (2011). Op. cit. p22.

[10] de Carvalho C N. *Geo-stories from these Places and People: Lousa*. Found
at:
http://www.naturtejo.com/ficheiros/conteudos/files/REPORT_77%20en.pdf

[11] Quoted in routes of Wolfram – Mines of Moimenta.
www.routesofwolfram.eu . These quotations are taken from the background
lecture to the *'Conference of the European project Routes of Wolfram'*
ISCET, Porto, 2013. Written and delivered by Professor Otilia Lage.

"When I was young, about twenty years old, I worked in the washing section. The rocks were crushed ... then the water and acid helped separate the tungsten. I say acid because all my clothes got burned." Alice Duarte da Silva.

Some mines had more advanced facilities. Vale de Gatas, which employed two thousand workers, provided medical services, a canteen, housing and a recreation centre; Regoufe invested in electricity, telephones and a road to reach the area. Yet even with these luxuries, life was still tough and dangerous:

"There were about 700 people working here ... Those who needed to earn came here. Those who lived near here came and went home every day. There were others who stayed here for years and even died here. Many galleries were damaged ... the water turned green from arsenic. The company has paid about $40,000 to the people for the two or three years they worked here ... electricity, telephone, roads. When they did not go to the mine they played cards, there were taverns ..."
Mr Joseph."[12]

There was also work for women and children who already lived in the communities, not necessarily any less dangerous. For example, they would undertake the dangerous task of preparing the dynamite used on a daily basis for the Argozolo mine.

An enlightened approach toward the workforce was rare. Investment was used principally to increase production or enhance access. However, Borralha, owned initially by France in pre-occupation days and then by the Nazi-controlled Vichy French regime, saw significant investment not just in machinery but also in education. Borralha was one of the few mining villages where children studied until at least age ten, allowing the sons of peasants to become engineers and economists:

"At the time the trade was a great school ... and the French were good and had knowledge ... they taught us the technologies ... Nothing was to be permanent ... here in Borralha – only the

---

[12] Ibid. Mines of Regoufe.

*school and the Casting building were made of stone ... It was
the great miracle of our region."*[13]

Kurt Dithmer

The complex manner in which the Germans gained legal access to the
Portuguese mines was embodied in the work of one man in particular,
Kurt Dithmer. He was a Director of one of the most important
European light-metal companies of the time, Gesellschaft für
Elektrometallurgie (GfE), whose President, Paul Grünfeld, was Jewish.
Consequently, the company had been Aryanised[14] in order for it to
trade with the Reich. Dithmer had been despatched to Portugal in his
mid-thirties in 1940 or 1941 (secret service files are uncertain), leaving
behind his wife and young son. His role was to head up the company's
operations in Portugal, particularly in relation to wolfram extraction
and export.

On arrival in Portugal, Dithmer began acquiring a controlling interest in
mines and mining companies, including Companhia Mineira do Norte
(Mining Company of Northern Portugal). From this time on until 1944,
he focused on their administration, attempting exports of wolfram and
the production in Portugal of certain light-alloy products. In order to do
this successfully, he needed the collaboration of fellow shareholders
who were influential Portuguese citizens. This included powerful
businessman Dr Souza Machado, who had the ear of the Minister of
Finance. The shareholders assisted in the purchase of land, properties,
and other assets, many of these paid for with credits from wolfram
shipments. In particular, Dithmer concentrated on investments likely to
attract the custom of people with influence or those susceptible to
influence – he bought hotels, sports clubs, football stadia and cinemas.
Many of these properties were in, or near, the northern coastal city of
Porto, as the companies found export from the more northerly mines
through Porto easier than through more distant Lisbon. To this end,

---

[13] Ibid. Mines of Borralha

[14] The removal of all Jews from company ownership so that the company
could legally be recognised as a supplier to the Third Reich.

Dithmer was responsible for the organisation of 'the German Group of Porto'.

There was another purpose to such acquisitions[15]: as the end of the war came into sight, German-owned properties and investments outside of Germany were considered a safer bet for post-war regeneration of wealth and power. Additionally, taking a controlling interest rather than outright control meant that, if things went wrong, other parties would be partly culpable. For example, Dithmer had a 38% personal stake in Companhia Mineira do Norte, the remaining 62% being shared among six carefully-chosen Portuguese collaborators. During 1940/41, it was the 10th largest mining company in the country and in 1942 employed 10,000 people across 79 separate mining concessions.[16]

By 1944, his fellow-investor Dr Machado, was making strenuous efforts to prevent the Portuguese authorities confiscating Dithmer's fixed assets and, when the war did come to an end, he endeavoured to prevent the repatriation of the German for trial. Dithmer had lived in the hope that, post-war, he could re-establish his business position through his connections with non-Nazi, former patrons.

At the end of the war, Dithmer was hiding in the Quinta dos Sonhos, an elegant country estate he owned near Porto. In post-war interrogation, he and his colleagues were to allege that his former company in Germany, GfE, had rightfully belonged to the Jewish owner and should not have been seized by the Nazis. Dithmer's business strategy worked: he remained free, continued to live in Portugal as a successful businessman with the mine remaining operational until 1953. Likewise, his fellow-investor Dr Machado was still involved in 1964 with a mining company in the African colony of Angola.

15

http://lawcollections.library.cornell.edu/bookreader/nur:01808/#page/1/mode/1up

[16] Figures from correspondence between author and Prof Otilia Lage.

Chapter 7

Social impact

If the volframistas, dazzled by the pleasures and riches of the moment, gave little thought to their own future, Lisbon's literati certainly did so. There was unease at the sudden increase in affluence and how this was being managed. Even dissident citizens, no supporters of Salazar's political view, agreed that a populace which was illiterate and unsophisticated was not prepared for a seismic shift in personal and community wealth. On 4 March 1942, the lead editorial of the opposition newspaper *Republica* even described the wolfram rush as an "illness" which promoted "egoism and the blindness of fate."[17] Such a view was reflected elsewhere in the topical discussion of the phenomenon in the press, in the cinema, in theatre reviews and in that reflection of personal grief and longing for past times, the music of the fado.

Irene Seligo was a German writer much-admired by Salazar for her short stories and he permitted her to stay on in Lisbon whilst other Germans were being deported. She wrote compellingly of life in the Beira region in 1941-42:

> *".... The effects of the wolfram fever among the simple people along the frontier, where the snow lies until May, where witches and sorcerers have more influence than the clergy, where the shepherds carry on a miniature but ceaseless war on wolves, and where those who work in the stony fields seldom eat their fill but were, for all that, industrious and contented until speculators enticed them away to look for a metal now so urgently required by a world at war. For a short time the frenzy of a California gold rush spread over the countryside."*[18]

---

[17] Wheeler, op cit. p115

[18] Seligo I. (1942). From *A day at Alcobaca* in *Delfina – short stories from a German journalist's life in wartime Lisbon*. Frankfurt: Societäts-verlag. Quoted in translation by Wheeler, op cit. p115.

Political intervention

Salazar was concerned about the mining phenomenon impacting on his grand plan for the slow but steady economic development of the country. It is no surprise that during the hostilities Salazar lost more sleep over the wolfram issue than any other matter.[19] On 5 June 1942, his radio broadcast to the nation referred to the "high price" of neutrality.

Earlier that year he had imposed official controls on the wolfram trade through the newly-established Metals Regulatory Commission. His threefold aim was to control prices, stop fossicking, and encourage fossickers to return to their traditional jobs *on* the land rather than below it. The Commission would also ensure, he hoped, that the Germans would receive their agreed quota. The intention had been, as the title suggests, to regulate supply, although it was also to help Portugal maintain neutrality. However, this concept was not shared by the belligerents – Germany simply thought it meant that they could buy more wolfram at a lower price; the Allies thought that it would bring some structure and order to the chaotic situation and reduce the costs of pre-emptive buying. In fact, the Commission was ultimately to disappoint all three stakeholders.

The Commission's main issues related to pricing and monitoring. Wolfram rose from 80 US cents in 1939 to 24 US dollars in early 1942, seemingly out of control with both belligerents gazumping each other. This astounding figure was to rise further and, of course, black market prices would take it even higher. Supplying both sides was always going to be difficult to regulate fully. Whilst it might be relatively straightforward for the Commission to oversee official supplies, those coming via the black-market were notoriously complex to calculate and monitor. The Germans were more desperate for wolfram than the Allies who could at least rely on obtaining ore from elsewhere in the globe. Linked to both the above factors, the Commission would bring greater law and order to the trade and thereby reduce the undermining of social structures that the illicit trade had damaged in the pursuit of short-term financial gain. A new wolfram mining export tax was introduced in

---

[19] Wheeler, op cit. p107

order to help pay for the increasing need to import essential foodstuffs
and fuel.

Rolling all these intended outcomes together, Salazar believed that he
had established a body which would defend his interpretation of
neutrality and enforce it for the world to see. However, real-world
economics meant that, quite naturally, the imposition of a tax merely
made illegal export even more enticing for the miners and their agents.
The figures for the tonnage of wolfram obtained by both sides are given
in the table below.

Year	UK / Allies	Germany	% received by Germany	Value by ton
1937	300 UK	155	5	80c per kilo
1940	3432 UK / 5235 Allies	1824	31	$13
1941	3845 Allies	1915	37.5	$24
1942	4588 Allies	1405	25	$1200
1943	6792 Allies	600	20	?
Feb-June 1944	2765	?	?	?
June-Dec 1944	?	150 (smuggled)	?	?

*Figure 25. Estimates of Portuguese wolfram (in tons)
obtained by Second World War belligerents.[20]*

These incomplete figures are difficult to verify for obvious reasons
given the illicit smuggling. Nor do they reflect the black market price
of £2,000 per ton in 1943 when the world market price was a mere
£330. Illegal practices confused the picture. For example, 'absorption'
was common. This involved taking 'free' wolfram produced near mines
and presenting it to the Portuguese authorities as part of the official
German figures. Likewise, some suppliers 'under-weighed' ore by

---

[20] British Chamber of Commerce in Portugal, 1945.

mixing the concentrate with earth; or by falsifying the figures recorded for official purposes.

Kay contends[21] that the free wolfram production was split 75% to 25% in favour of Germany and that the belligerents sold to the Commission at £800 a ton and bought back at £1,200, plus an export tax of £300 a ton. On the basis of these figures, the Portuguese government was making £700 on each ton traded – a significant percentage of the total export value.

The Luso-German Accord of January 1942 was a short-term, one-year agreement when Germany was at its most desperate for wolfram and sorely needed to legitimatise as much supply as possible. In return for Germany supplying steel, coal and fertiliser, Portugal would supply 2,800 tons of wolfram (a significant increase over the previous year), including all the wolfram from German-owned mines and half of the 'free' wolfram. There were unintended consequences surrounding the supply of the latter. The situation led to 'pre-emptive buying' on both sides, often at extortionate prices simply to prevent the enemy from getting further supplies. The issue became 'market share at any price'. A telling example of the Germans' desperation is the story of a wolfram agent who mistakenly placed the decimal point for the value of the sale in the wrong place. He worried over this error, petrified that it would be interpreted as trying to swindle the Germans and that he would be shot. When the Germans paid in full without quibbling (paying ten times as much as they should have), his relief was immense.[22]

Although the Allies calculated that Germany needed 3,500 tons a year to satisfy industrial and munitions needs, they were unable to contest Portugal supplying the agreed quota so, six months later, in August 1942 the Allies devised their own one-year agreement with Portugal. This limited German supplies to the existing 2,800 tons but released all the recognised wolfram from British-owned mines and a portion of the free wolfram. Coming as it did in the Allies' darkest year of 1942, this

---

[21] Kay, op cit. p178.

[22] As recounted in this video clip
https://www.youtube.com/watch?v=BN_BGers32Q

agreement provided some relief, but it was short-lived. 1943 saw an unprecedented heatwave in Portugal which had a severe effect on agricultural harvests. Perhaps fearful of the cost of importing more food supplies, by the end of 1943 Salazar had entered into yet another wolfram agreement with Germany. Simultaneously, he was seeking price reductions from the Allies in fuel products and ammonium sulphate. When these were refused, Salazar likewise refused to increase the number of export licences to the Allies.

Wheeler estimates[23] that Britain and the US spent at least $116 million ($1.6 billion in today's value) during 1942-1944 (including pre-emptive purchases), whilst Kay estimates[24] the total Allied cost of wartime wolfram from the Iberian Peninsula as $170 million. These are staggering figures which, if accurate, underline how short-term the strategies were becoming.

With these agreements in place, Germany still attempted to smuggle beyond their allocated tonnages between 1942 and 1944, partly in response to a strong feeling that they were not receiving their full official allocations. Angry letters of 'undiplomatic tone' were sent by German representatives to the Portuguese government in 1942, and a tense relationship continued over several years. In January 1944, the British attempted a complete embargo on wolfram supplies to Germany, arguing that the country was getting nearly all its requirements from Portugal and that this was unnecessarily prolonging the war. This was a significant argument at a time when the balance of the war was shifting in favour of the Allies. By May 1945, Portugal had passed Law 34,600, which eventually froze all German assets in Portugal. When the D-Day landings cut off all overland supply routes through France that summer, the demand for and the value of wolfram plummeted.

As with so much exploration, extraction and refining of natural resources, there is a break-even point for operators. This rapid and irreversible plunge in demand and prices brought about the desertion of many mines and surrounding communities, including the massive

---

[23] Wheeler, op cit p121

[24] Kay, op cit p180.

Panasqueira operation. Only with the outbreak of another international war, the Korean War (1950-1953), were demand and prices to rise sufficiently for the mine to re-open profitably – along with others which had closed at Vale das Gatas and Casaio.

The mining area today

Today, many of the mines and their communities lie abandoned, as do the roads approaching them. Photographs of the Rio de Frades area are included in Chapter 9, and further images can be found on the excellent website *Emma's House in Portugal*[25] or the *Ghost Mines* film[26]. Panasqueira remains very active, now owned and operated profitably by the Chinese company Sojitz Beralt Tin & Wolfram (Portugal) S.A.

Figure 26. Image of derelict Barroca Grande mining village serving Panasqueira mine.

The region is trying hard to regenerate itself as a tourist base, particularly for Nordic athletes, because of its proximity to the nearby

[25] http://www.emmashouseinportugal.com/living-in-portugal/volframio-portugal-in-ww2/

[26] https://www.youtube.com/watch?v=RGdoibk43ZY

Chapter 7

Serra de Estrala Natural Park with its ski slopes, river beaches, hiking, fishing and suitability for off-road driving and biking. Some local entrepreneurs wish to re-open the mines as a tourist attraction, allowing visitors to descend to the working stalls, just as they can in Britain at the National Coal Mining Museum in Wakefield or at Big Pit in Blaenavon, South Wales. Individual derelict houses, in terraces of eight properties, in the adjoining mining village, were on sale in Spring 2015 for just €4,200 each in an attempt to create a leisure village. The sales pitch of the estate agents does not overcome the fact that the Panasqueira area is remote, with cold, snowy winters and occasional severe flooding in the valleys after torrential rain. Only ghostly echoes of the brief, frenzied wartime activities remain.

Chapter 8
Gold Laundering

Chapter 3 illustrated that Dr Salazar was a complex man driven by equally complex values. His harsh view of his fellow citizens was underpinned by a fervently-held view of what he believed was best for the nation. Supplying both sides of belligerents with wolfram and other goods was an economic coup but, unsurprisingly, Salazar was determined to gain the best price and method of payment from each side in order to attain his Estado Novo.

Goods purchased by Britain were paid for via a tripartite agreement between Britain, Spain and Portugal, set up in July 1940 whereby Britain provided credit notes against Sterling for the duration of the war. The underlying idea was that, whilst Portugal gained no immediate benefit from the sales, it would build up its reserve of future spending potential. Indeed, by the end of the war the credit note reserve was £80 million[1], all of which Portugal duly spent on British goods. This was a seemingly straightforward agreement, although there were complications along the way.

Whilst Salazar trusted Britain to keep its word as far as credit notes were concerned, he did not trust the Nazis to do the same. Consequently, sales agreements for products to the Nazis were far more complex, even though a cornerstone of Salazar's neutral position was that both sides should be provided with equal amounts of goods. In order for Salazar to be assured that there was no direct audit trail of gold from Germany to Portugal, sales to the Nazis became a complex three-way web which also involved fellow neutral state, Switzerland.

The German economic war went through three distinct phases. Until June 1940, Germany paid through exchanged goods. However, the Nazi demand for wolfram far exceeded what Portugal with its limited industrial economic base needed in return. Additionally, as the war progressed, Germany needed to keep substantial stocks of its

---

[1] Kay H. (1970). Op cit. p172

Chapter 8

machinery and vehicle production to assist directly in its own war efforts. There was clearly a shortfall which needed to be paid for by other means. The German currency of the day, the Reichsmark, had only a paper value and, of course, was considerably overvalued and subject to forged notes produced in the printing presses of Nazi-occupied countries. Images of German citizens desperately taking wheelbarrows full of Reichsmarks to buy their groceries are part of the visual history of Germany's pre-war days and the image remained strong, particularly for an economist like Salazar. He was rightly concerned about the value of the Reichsmark which, unlike Sterling, was not a currency backed by gold.

The second phase of the economic war came after the fall of France in 1940 when Portugal needed coal and fertiliser. British shipping was now fully committed to transatlantic convoys or merchant shipping that directly supported the war effort. By contrast, Germany could supply Portugal with goods by rail via occupied France and fascist-leaning Spain. This option was not the easiest though, particularly for bulky cargo – Portugal and Spain's Iberian rail system had a separate gauge from the rest of mainland Europe, necessitating switching goods to different rolling stock at the French-Spanish border. This was a cumbersome and time-consuming process – and remains an irritant to this day for passengers who still have to change between high-speed trains with standard-gauge and older Iberian-gauge trains.

After Pearl Harbor in 1941, with the USA's entry to the war, Portugal's gold reserves (which had been sent to New York for safe-keeping) were frozen for the duration of the conflict and Salazar was keen to develop separate reserves. Consequently, gold became the means of payment for wolfram and other goods. By this stage of the war, Portugal had become the principal source of wolfram for Germany as Hitler's misguided assault on Russia had cut off permanently the alternative, Siberian reserves. This third and final phase of the economic war coincided with the agreement referred to in Chapter 7 about the wolfram purchase programme which sought to regulate wolfram sales on an equitable basis and from recognised mines. Between 1941 and 1944, Portugal collected 3,834,134,000 escudos from Germany, but the

currency value was actually translated into 128.8 metric tons of gold.[2]
About two-thirds of this came via Swiss banks.

Sources of the gold

On the surface of it, demanding security of payment in gold seems
innocent enough. But where had it come from? Nazi gold stock has
become a notorious part of the history of the Second World War in its
own right and the role of the Swiss banks in supplying it has also been
the subject of much subsequent investigation. So-called 'Nazi gold'
came from a number of sources. Firstly, there were the confiscated
reserves of the central banks of countries overrun by the Nazis. Louca
(op. cit.) calculates the value of these reserves as being $102,600,000
from Austria, $222,900,000 from Belgium and $163,800,000 from
Holland. All these central bank vaults were plundered in order to
release the gold for Nazi purposes, in the same way that art collections
from public buildings were also looted.

Additionally, gold reserves from other countries which had been
annexed or overrun were plundered, plus private individuals' assets, to
a value of $929,900,000. These are minimal estimates and include, of
course, the value of the metal obtained from Holocaust victims. The
latter is naturally a particularly harrowing aspect of the story, as it
involved not just plundering the assets held in banks, private vaults or
safes but also from victims' bodies. *"Looting monetary gold was one
thing – stealing it from individuals, from victims, is another."*[3] Part of
the dehumanising process of incarceration in concentration camps lay
in not just being separated from family members, being starved, kept in
primitive conditions, being branded with an identity number and being
humiliated by extreme forced labour, but also to have personal
possessions taken so that there was no sense of identity, memories or of

---

[2] Louca A. *Nazigold für Portugal: Hitler und Salazar*. Wien: Holzhausen.
2002. 281.

[3] Louca A. Interview in article in *New York Times*, 10 January 1997 by
Simons M. Nazi Gold and Portugal's Murky Role. Available at:
www.nytimes.com/1997/01/10/world/nazi-gold-and-portugal-s-murky-
role.html?pagewanted=2

Chapter 8

a future outside the camp.[4] Wedding rings, jewellery, cigarette cases, spectacle frames, pocket and wristwatches were all taken for their precious metals. So too were gold teeth, forcibly extracted from live inmates. Dead bodies were plundered for missing implants – fillings, bridges and crowns. The grim task of the dental crews is vividly outlined below, as told by SS Obersturmführer Kurt Gerstein to a Swedish diplomat in August 1942 at Belzec extermination camp:

> *Up to that moment, the people shut up in those four crowded chambers were still alive, four times 750 persons, in four times 45 cubic meters (sic). Another 25 minutes elapsed. Many were already dead, that could be seen through the small window, because an electric lamp inside lit up the chamber for a few moments. After 28 minutes, only a few were still alive. Finally, after 32 minutes, all were dead ... Dentists then hammered out the gold teeth, bridges and crowns. In the midst of them stood Captain Wirth. He was in his element, and, showing me a large can full of teeth, he said: "See for yourself, the weight of that gold! It's only from yesterday and the day before. You can't imagine what we find everyday – dollars, diamonds, gold. You'll see for yourself!"[5]*

The gold collected at the camps was despatched to the Reichsbank for laundering under the false name of Max Heiliger to be melted down for bullion. 'Heiliger' means 'saint' in German and was a distasteful

---

[4] This denial of human hope is vividly and emotionally encapsulated in the powerful design of the Holocaust Memorial in Berlin. From a distance it appears to be an unimaginative series of concrete blocks, yet its power overwhelms you as soon as you walk into it. The helpless sense of there being no escape, of entrapment and of dehumanisation is precisely what the designers envisaged.

[5] Stackleberg R & Winkle S A. (2002). *The Nazi Sourcebook: An Anthology of Texts*. London: Routledge. p354. Extract available online at: http://en.m.wikipedia.org/wiki/Extermination_camp

attempt at humour, just as Sobibor camp's one-way path to the gas chambers was called Himmelstrasse (Heaven Street). Much of the gold was stored in the Merkers salt mine in Thuringia (see below).

Figure 27. Gold stored in the Merkers salt mine, April 1945.

Such illicit actions of using victim gold (although not the hideous, full detail) were becoming known to the Allies because they carefully monitored evidence of gold transactions in Lisbon, keeping a tally at the British Embassy. In July 1943, the BBC made it quite clear in a broadcast to Lisbon that all gold bearing German insignia would be considered as stolen. This aroused concern among the Lisbon dealers who feared for their own position after the war. They demanded that the national bank, the Bank of Portugal, should no longer hold ingots with German insignia and should exchange them forthwith for those with different insignia. Porto, with its smelting facilities, became a popular haunt of dealers wishing to convert their own holdings. The Bank of Portugal did not capitulate though and their inaction was to have ramifications many years later. However, the Nazis began to see a way around this problem and started to export ingots by another means to Portugal.

Figure 28. Generals Eisenhower and Bradley examining suitcases of gold, gold rings and teeth, December 1945.

D-Day and the closing stages of the war

As the Allies prepared in secret for Operation Overlord (the code name given to the Normandy D-Day landings in June 1944) the gold trade was to experience further repercussions. Instead of being destined for the Bank of Portugal, four shipments of Nazi gold – shipped in four stages of 80 kilos each across a one-week period in the summer of 1944 – were sent to the German Embassy in Lisbon, including by diplomatic pouch. The timing was just weeks after the D-Day landings in France and could be seen as a desperate attempt to get gold out of Germany, particularly as Switzerland had refused to accept any further supply after the failed attempt on Hitler's life in July 1944. The Anglo-American Safehaven Program to identify and locate looted gold had already been established as a preventative measure to fund future Nazi actions. By this time, with the Allied forces now established in mainland Europe, land deliveries of wolfram were impossible. Salazar recognised this and, with pressure from the Allies, an agreement to stop all exports to Germany was reached. Salazar was coming to realise that the Allies would be victorious, although he still hoped for a negotiated settlement – principally because he was fearful of the Russian, Communist influence in post-war mainland Europe.

A key player in the gold market was the Banco Espírito Santo, run by its eponymous head, Ricardo. As seen in Chapter 4, he had the ear of Salazar when hosting the Duke of Windsor at his home earlier in the war and he retained his close connections with the government. When, in 1944, as part of the clamp-down on wolfram and other trade with Germany, America called for Reichsbank accounts to be transferred elsewhere, his autocratic power made his bank a more nimble outfit than the cumbersome, bureaucratic structure of other banks, and he could be seen to be preparing for business in a post-war world. Indeed, Banco Espírito Santo continued to trade until August 2014 after the EU bail-out of Portugal, when it was split into two separate banks under changed names to distinguish the 'good' bank from the one with 'toxic assets'. The 'good' bank is called Novo Bank; the 'toxic' bank is, apparently[6], nameless to the public.

The influx of gold into Portugal (with no compensatory export trade to Germany), led to complaints by the German Embassy in July 1944 about the fall in its price. Berlin also suspected[7] that this was partly due to the unintended consequence of actions in Hungary. An ally of Germany, Hungary had been making noises about withdrawing from the war, resulting in the German occupation of the country from March 1944. This occupation had included taking over the running of the second largest heavy industry concern in Europe, the Manfred Weiss works, which was owned by several wealthy Jewish families. In order to be eligible for German government orders and thus remain in business, the company had to undergo 'Aryanisation'[8], so the Jewish owners and their extended families were ousted, incarcerated and then finally permitted to leave Hungary for Lisbon in June 1944. Thirty-two of the forty-four family members arrived as refugees, many en-route to the USA. Whilst they denied bringing gold to Lisbon, the word in Germany was that they had brought much of their considerable wealth with them in the form of ingots and gold jewellery. However, even if

---

[6] According to *City of Spies* tour guide by Lisbon Walks.

[7] Simons M. (op. cit.)

[8] Excerpt from the Memoirs of George Hoff, Legal Counsel. The Manfred Weiss – SS Deal of 1944. *Hungarian Studies* 7/1-2. 1991/92. Available at: www.epa.oszkhu p26.

true, it is unlikely that this influx would have had as significant an impact on the gold price as the wider issue of Allied military presence on European soil preventing its transit.

Post-war tracing of gold

Once the war was over, considerable investigative attempts were undertaken to identify what happened to the Nazi gold deposited in Portugal (and other countries). The total value of looted gold was calculated to be somewhere between $545-550 million.[9] Investigations were linked not just to seeking reparation for the plundered metal, but also to determining the complicity of Swiss banks in laundering ill-gotten gold. Such a focus gained further momentum with the establishment of the State of Israel and, in particular, the relentless activity of the Simon Wiesenthal Center in tracking down Nazis who had escaped the Nuremburg War Crimes trials, often fleeing from Spain to South America.

Post-war, Allied demands included that Portugal repay at least forty-four tons. Despite fierce censorship obscuring government deals right up until Salazar's death, it is now apparent that Lisbon secretly began to sell off gold deposits, particularly in the Far East via its territory of Macao. Some of these bars bore the Dutch seal, others the Nazi swastika. Likewise, the Bank of Portugal did not reveal the extent of its involvement and, even as late as 1997, a bank official noted that it still had "two or three"[10] gold bars stamped with swastikas and stated that they were merely "kept as curiosities".

Nearly a decade after the end of the gold transit era of the war, in 1953, the Allies, via the Allied Tripartite Commission, gave up the pursuit of gold and settled on just four of the calculated forty-four tons being returned. One of the problems encountered by investigators was the intransigence of Swiss banks who argued that whilst it might be known that a prisoner entered a death camp, there was inconclusive evidence

---

[9] British Ministry of Economic Warfare figures quoted in Lochery, op. cit., p202.

[10] New York Times, op. cit.

of death – simply that there was no record of their emerging alive from the camp.[11] The report commissioned by President Clinton into the actions of neutral countries in the Second World War argued in 1998 that, close to the end of the twentieth century, now was the time to make reparations for "this lingering ledger of grief"[12] unresolved from the middle of the century. In response, the 1999 Portuguese official commission report retorted that, as the nation had been free to trade with both sides and there was no evidence that it had knowingly dealt in looted gold, there was no moral obligation for repayment to Holocaust or other Nazi victims.

The story does not end there. During Salazar's student days at Coimbra University, in nearby Fatima, three peasant children had claimed to see apparitions of the Virgin Mary (who is revered in Roman Catholicism). A shrine was established, attracting millions of devout believers annually, and in 1982 extensive refurbishment was undertaken, paid for by the sale of gold ingots held by the shrine's authorities. It was discovered that these ingots had Nazi insignia and the Rector of the shrine admitted that he had observed the insignia in 1976, and thought that they were "curious" but took no action.[13]

---

[11] *"All we know is that the deceased was last seen entering a concentration camp and is not known to have ever emerged."* Attributed to Paul Guggenheim, a Swiss lawyer assisting the claimants at a meeting in Bern, 17 November, 1952. Quoted in Bower T. (1997). *Nazi Gold*. London: HarperCollins.

[12] Eizenstat SE & Slany W. *US and Allied Wartime and Postwar Relations and Negotiations with Argentina, Portugal, Spain, Sweden and Turkey on Looted Gold and German External Assets and US Concerns About the Fate of the Wartime Ustasha Treasury*. Supplement to the Preliminary Study. Washington DC. 1998. Extract from Foreword.

[13] Associated Press report cited in Tuscaloosa News, 5 May 2000. Shrine says it owned Nazi gold. Available at: http://news.google.com/newspapers?nid=1817&dat=20000505&id=6jodAAA AIBAJ&sjid=CKYEAAAAIBAJ&pg=5466,538841

Chapter 8

Another lingering question remains. Why did Salazar allow the gold to sit in the vaults of the Bank of Portugal rather than using it to enhance the nation's infrastructure? As we saw in Chapter 3, his view of his subjects was that they were not yet ready for significant social change. Whilst he was already investing in road, rail and port infrastructure – this was not true to any significant degree in education, whose transformative quality risked changing the character and expectations of people. Was stockpiling gold a clever but failed political ploy awaiting price-rise upon peace? This is untenable because gold prices tend to rise in periods of warfare when goods are scarce and there is uncertainty. Indeed prices do not necessarily rise in an orderly, predictable manner but can soar unpredictably. The optimal time for Salazar to sell would have been in 1941, before the US placed an embargo on Portuguese trade.[14] More likely, it was simply a wasted economic opportunity; with Salazar unable to decide how best to spend the gold whilst still retaining the distinctive character of his nation.

The essence of the general question on the purpose of money is perhaps asked innocently, yet astutely, by the child Paul Dombey in Dickens's eponymous novel, *Dombey and Son*:

> *'Papa! What's money?'*
>
> *The abrupt question had such immediate reference to the subject of Mr Dombey's thoughts, that Mr Dombey was quite disconcerted.*
>
> *'What is money, Paul?' he answered. 'Money?'*
>
> *'Yes,' said the child, laying his hands upon the elbows of his little chair, and turning the old face up towards Mr Dombey's; 'what is money?'*
>
> *Mr Dombey was in a difficulty. He would have liked to give him some explanation involving the terms circulating-medium, currency, depreciation of currency, paper, bullion, rates of*

---

[14] The renowned economist Milton Friedman shows that international gold prices dipped in the latter part of the war, rising only in in 1948 to early war levels. Friedman M. (1980). *World War 11 Inflation*. Washington, D.C. National Bureau of Economic Research. http://www.nber.org/chapters/c11389.pdf

exchange, value of precious metals in the market, and so forth; but looking down at the little chair, and seeing what a long way down it was, he answered: 'Gold, and silver, and copper. Guineas, shillings, half-pence. You know what they are?'

'Oh yes, I know what they are,' said Paul. 'I don't mean that, Papa. I mean what's money after all?'

Heaven and Earth, how old his face was as he turned it up again towards his father's!

'What is money after all!' said Mr Dombey, backing his chair a little, that he might the better gaze in sheer amazement at the presumptuous atom that propounded such an inquiry.

'I mean, Papa, what can it do?' returned Paul, folding his arms (they were hardly long enough to fold), and looking at the fire, and up at him, and at the fire, and up at him again.

Mr Dombey drew his chair back to its former place, and patted him on the head. 'You'll know better by-and-by, my man,' he said. 'Money, Paul, can do anything.' He took hold of the little hand, and beat it softly against one of his own, as he said so.

But Paul got his hand free as soon as he could; and rubbing it gently to and fro on the elbow of his chair, as if his wit were in the palm, and he were sharpening it – and looking at the fire again, as though the fire had been his adviser and prompter – repeated, after a short pause:

'Anything, Papa?'

'Yes. Anything—almost,' said Mr Dombey.

'Anything means everything, don't it, Papa?' asked his son: not observing, or possibly not understanding, the qualification.

'It includes it: yes,' said Mr Dombey.

'Why didn't money save me my Mama?' returned the child. 'It isn't cruel, is it?'[15]

---

[15] Dickens C. (1848). *Dombey and Sons*, Chapter 8. London: Bradbury and Evans.

Chapter 8

The significance of this quotation became clear during a visit by the author to the Headquarters of the Bank of Portugal in the spring of 2015, which revealed that information about wartime gold reserves still does not flow freely. Questions on where it had been stored were met with polite but insistent shrugs of the shoulders, that *if* gold had ever been stored there it was long ago and that it was not the bank's policy to ever discuss such matters. This was despite a group of tourists on a *City of Spies* walk standing directly opposite the bank entrance. They were being informed by the guide of the bank's involvement in wartime gold transactions. The bank is, however, currently in the process of establishing its 'Money Museum' in an adjoining disused church, although no reference is made in the publicity to wartime gold. Interestingly, the museum wall contains both an edited version of the Dickens quotation above, and also a definition of money in answer to young Paul's question.

> *"Money is an abstract value or an object which serves as a means of exchange, measure and a store of value for a group, community or society. It reflects a system of equivalence between goods and services. If money is to be able to fulfil its functions, it must be easy to carry, durable, divisible, socially accepted and have a stable value."* (Definition used in Bank of Portugal Money Museum)

Portugal's role in, and profit from, the war, revolving around the shadowy history of the exchange of wolfram for Nazi gold, continues to draw questions – about openness and transparency regarding national assets and the deployment of such wealth to benefit the populace. In the next chapter, we'll look at the impact of these matters on post-war Portugal.

Chapter 9
Post-Wolfram Dark Days

Whilst Victory in Europe (VE) was celebrated in May 1945, the war would continue outside the European theatre until the defeat of the Japanese in September that year.

VE celebrations in Portugal were mixed. Whilst the population generally was delighted to see the end of the privations associated with war, the future was uncertain. Many politicians and citizens across Europe were aghast that Salazar was the only world leader to send a note of condolence to Germany on the death of Hitler.

Celebrations in Rossio Square were closely monitored by the PVDE who suppressed any dissident behaviour. This led to some unusual activities among the crowd. The Portuguese language has two words for red – 'encarnado' and 'vermelho'. Supporters of Benfica Football Club, who would have formed a large proportion of the crowd, are known as 'encarnados'; Communist sympathisers are associated with 'vermelho'. The public photographs outside the British Embassy show Lisboans holding sticks but with no coloured flag attached to them, lest their support for Benfica be interpreted as Communist sympathy. It is an odd and telling image once you notice the omissions and, had there been red flags, the secret police would certainly have been tracking down the offenders.

Abandoned mines and villages

For many citizens in Portugal, particularly those involved directly in the wolfram rush, the closing stages of the war had come as a surprise. Given the urgency and fervour with which wolfram had been sought, mined, processed, transported and traded either legally or through smuggling, it seemed incomprehensible to the miners and other workers that this vital and lucrative work should come to a sudden end. Many of them were uneducated labourers, not privy to the ways of the world or to international affairs. To them, it was a mystery how these foreign countries had changed their minds so quickly. Salazar's embargo on the export of wolfram, the sudden loss of interest by the Germans once France had been liberated (thus preventing any rail or

Chapter 9

road route to the German border), and the plummeting value of the hard-won mineral were puzzling. The old folk-song sung in the early 1940s about the wealth brought about by wolfram ore now rang hollow:

> *"Eu fui ao Porto, levar minério para vender*
> *Para baixo fui de comboio*
> *Para cima de carro*
> *Não quero saber."*

In translation:

> *"I went to Oporto, with ore to sell*
> *went down by trail*
> *up by car*
> *I do not care."*[1]

Suddenly, life had changed. The slashed prices for wolfram meant that it was no longer economic to extract and process the ore from many mines. The mining facilities were mothballed, some of them permanently, or at least until the outbreak of the Korean War at the start of the next decade when demand for munitions would return. Even then, only the most prolific mines with the lowest operating overheads would again become commercial enterprises.

It wasn't just the work facilities which stopped operations. Many of the villages, particularly those which had attracted migrant workers from elsewhere in Portugal, suffered from the exodus of workers. Additionally, freelance fossickers working small wolfram stakes simply upped sticks and returned to their homes. If there was no wolfram business, there was no work. This phenomenon would impact on the whole supply chain – the butcher, the baker and the candlestick maker. In particular, it impacted on the innkeepers and bartenders who had made a good living out of providing alcohol, company and relaxation to the exhausted miners eager to quench their thirsts. Now there was nothing.

---

[1] Quoted by Lage. (2011). op. cit.

Where the workers comprised either single men or husbands who had left their home area to find work to support their families, the consequent unemployment was simply transferred from the Beira region to other areas of Portugal. Given the low levels of urbanisation in Portugal, this reverse migration resulted in spreading unemployment more thinly across the nation. But where the workers had been indigenous to the Beira, with families depending on their earnings, the ensuing poverty stayed in the region. There was little prospect of other employment, save poorly-paid peasant farm labouring which they had left in favour of becoming volframistas. Those local people previously involved in hosting and providing for the British or German wolfram agents, mining engineers or traders were also out of a job. Few foreigners needed to stay in the often inhospitable territory.

The photographs tell their own story: run-down domestic properties, derelict mine buildings, deserted villages, overgrown pathways and roads. Some areas had become polluted, the ground despoiled with copper-coloured mining waste, rivers poisoned by arsenic, dead fish floating on the surface until eventually the river supported no life at all. Photographic images show[2] individuals sitting on their front doorstep, wistfully gazing into space. Do they lack aspirations or the wherewithal to improve their lot? Do they simply feel trapped by circumstances which they have no power to change? These images are reminiscent of those moving photographs of the Oklahoma Dustbowl of the 1930s, captured also so vividly in fiction by John Steinbeck's novel *The Grapes of Wrath*.

---

[2] www.routesofwolfram.eu. An EU-funded project to raise awareness of the wolfram trade in Portugal.

Figure 29. Image of deserted Rio de Frades mining village.

Figure 30. Image of deserted Rio de Frades mining village.

Oral histories convey the sense of poverty affecting the area, particularly as local villagers watched food supplies passing in rail wagons on a railway originally built to transport ore:

> *"... in 1945 cereal was shipped directly for Tua to Barca d'Alva and then to Spain .... and we would eat crumbs."*

> *"... in 1945, because of the famine we had nothing to eat ... it was rations ... there were a few watermills upriver ... and Isabel, the baker, would go to Vilarinho das Azenhas and bring back bread from Cachão to sell and eat ... a little rye bread cost a lot of money..."* [3]

At a strategic level, this phenomenon is what many Lisbon politicians had been fearing – that the work would dry up, that there would be a consequent catastrophic impact on the economy of the country and that the uneducated, unemployed workers would become a threat to the

---

[3] Reminiscences of local people, interviewed 2011. Quoted in Lage. (2011). op. cit. p23.

stability of the Estado Novo. The dispossessed and unemployed were now spread across the nation, making it more difficult for the secret police to monitor, yet potentially allowing the malcontents to fall into the hands of Communist agitators. During the war, Salazar had used the wealth gained from wolfram only modestly to improve the nation's infrastructure. Much of this investment had been in the 1930s to build the ports, roads and railways crucial for export and in maintaining trading links with Portugal's colonies. In this respect, Salazar had been successful but there had been less focus on diversifying the economic base of the nation or in upskilling the populace. As we have seen, Salazar's paternalistic view of his nation and its subjects meant that he was acutely afraid of too much change too quickly. Much of the gold remained securely in the vaults of the Bank of Portugal for unspecified future use.

Figure 31. Image of deserted Rio de Frades mining village.

Portugal starts looking to a brighter future

Matters started to improve from 1960 but this still left fifteen years of misery, particularly the first five years – until 1950 – when the economy and the country were virtually stagnant. The simple truth was that, whilst the country had grown very rich under Salazar's neutral policy, growth remained weak. Even by 1950, low-level agriculture occupied 50% of the workforce yet yielded only 25% of the nation's income.[4]

Abroad, the havoc of the post-wolfram era was acknowledged. *The Economist* described this period as characterised by:

> *"Mines wrecked by ruthless methods, miners too enriched by clandestine profits to return to the service of the reputable concerns, and a price level of some 26 escudos per kilo as against 650 at the wartime peak."*[5]

For philosophical reasons, Portugal initially declined the offer in 1947 of US Aid made under the Marshall Plan to reinvigorate European economies, provided that this was done in a cooperative, strategic manner. As in pre-war days, Salazar still felt that the acceptance of assistance from integrationist, non-Catholic states would taint the purity of his national dream. Given the source of Nazi gold, which he had readily accepted in wartime, this rejection had more than a whiff of sanctimonious hypocrisy. A year later, reason prevailed and Salazar made the first tentative overtures via his Ambassador, Rui Teixeira Guerra, to maximise access to such funds.

This development signalled the first departure from the previously strict economic policy of Salazar, and brought in an influential new generation of politicians with a background in economics. In a sense it was a backhanded compliment to his successes, given that Salazar's own initial career at Coimbra University represented the first ever appointment in the nation of a Lecturer in Economics. By now there were more economists in the government and in positions of influence, and the Portuguese economy started to take off in the 1960s. How this growth developed, we will examine in the final chapter of the book.

---

[4] Gallagher T. (1982). *Portugal: A Twentieth Century Interpretation.* Manchester: Manchester University Press

[5] 'Portugal: A Special Survey'. *The Economist*. April 17, 1954. p235.

Chapter 10
Modern Portugal

With the end of hostilities, Portugal was free to align itself with whoever it wished or to plough its own furrow, although the nature of the financial agreement with Britain meant that it was tied into this trading partnership.

The period did not start well for relations with Britain, principally because of Salazar's letter of condolence to Germany on the death of Hitler, with flags on public buildings flying at half-mast to signify the government's mourning. Despite this ill-feeling, Churchill chose to spend some time recovering his health on the island of Madeira on the recommendation of the British Consul, Bryce Nairn, as somewhere which would be, "warm, paintable, bathable, comfortable and flowery". Churchill stayed in a suite at Reid's Hotel (the favoured haunt of aristocrats from around the world). Greeted by locals and the British ex-pat community alike as "the man who saved the world", he was famously photographed painting in the local fishing village of Camara de Lobos, before recovering sufficiently to fight and win the 1951 election.

The evolution of wartime Portugal into a modern state has been a slow and, at times, painful process politically, economically and culturally. A number of factors have contributed to this rocky transition. Key aspects of Salazar's dictatorial view, as we have seen, involved retaining his country in an unsullied state and his distrust of international bodies. This perspective slowly started to change, particularly from 1960.

Immediately after the war, the dictator had been shocked by Churchill's British election defeat and was fearful of the socialist government of the victor, Clement Attlee. Aware that he too had to implement change at home, Salazar announced elections with some modest form of opposition allowed. However, just prior to the November 1945 elections, it seems that old habits were to die hard and his secret police crushed any opposition party activists planning to stand.[1] The 1946 wheat harvest and sardine catch had also been disastrous[2] and threatened the economic stability of the nation.

Bad news continued from across the globe. 1947 marked the independence of India from the British Empire, a distasteful development for Salazar who feared that such heretical actions might influence the island of Goa in the Indian Ocean. Whilst the Portuguese leader "embraced the concept of a Pan-Lusitanian community, geographically scattered but spiritually united"[3], the thought of independence and governmental divorce from Portugal was unthinkable. By 1949, when the nation was admitted to the United Nations (the organisation previously so detested by Salazar), the country made its presence known by fighting against the decolonisation process enshrined in Chapter XI of the UN Charter, citing legalistic exemptions. Such opposition to the self-determination, particularly of its African colonies, was to exact a heavy price for many years to come.

African wars

Deeply rooted in modern Portuguese history are the bloody years of guerrilla warfare from 1961-1974 in Africa, particularly in Angola and Mozambique. We saw, in Chapter 3, how Salazar had promoted the size of these two colonies as representing that 'Portugal was not a small country'. Surrounded by nations gaining their independence, these African colonies were locked in a lengthy, ferocious war both internally and against Portugal. For Angola, the war of independence ended only after the toppling of the Estado Novo in 1974, with full independence being gained in 1975 after Salazar's death. Angola's victory nevertheless plunged it into years of civil conflict. In Mozambique, on the east coast of Africa, the Marxist-Leninist Front for the Liberation of Mozambique (FRELIMO) movement battled Portuguese militia.

---

[1] Lochery. op cit. p233.

[2] Kay. op cit. p182

[3] Kay. op cit. p212

Likewise, Mozambique gained independence in 1974 with the military overthrow in Lisbon of the Estado Novo. It is deeply ironic that Salazar saved the lives of many young men by keeping his nation out of the Second World War, yet sent so many conscripts from the next generation to their deaths in Africa in a wasted effort to stem the tide of independence.[4]

Salazar's more outward-looking stance 1960s

Portugal was one of the founder members of the European Free Trade Association (EFTA) which opened up trading links with member states Austria, Denmark, Norway, Sweden, Switzerland and the UK. The world was becoming high-tech: scientific, electronic and medical advances made Salazar realise that this was the way to progress economically. Consequently, he instituted investment in industries which would assist such development. Whilst the age-old artisan businesses continued, they were accompanied by the rise of large, corporatist conglomerates in cement, petrochemicals and agrichemicals. These entities were often in the hands of families sympathetic to Estado Novo's aims, and it is estimated[5] that a mere ten families owned the nation's leading 170 companies and controlled 53% of its wealth.

In 1986, the country became part of that much larger organisation, the European Union. Set up originally to maintain peace across Europe, the EU has provided many economic and cultural benefits to Portugal, including access to regional funding, development of its scientific, research and development base, as well as the free movement of citizens. EU membership encouraged a great deal of inward investment into advanced industry. For example, the Volkswagen Sharan, Scirocco, Eos and the SEAT Alhambra are assembled at the huge AutoEuropa plant in Palmela outside Lisbon, from where they are

---

[4] A further irony lies in the soldiers of the African Wars being equipped with old, yet still "highly efficient German Mauser weaponry" bought as part of the Second World War neutral trade to fight this "stupid African war". Quoted by a former soldier, now Concierge at the Palácio hotel.

[5] Jepson T. (2001, 2nd ed.). *Explorer Portugal*. Basingstoke: AA

exported globally; whilst the home-grown Salvador Caetano conglomerate (one of those founded in the post-war period) builds and exports buses, some of which grace British roads in National Express livery.

A wonderful illustration of the combination of the old and the new nation was demonstrated in NASA's decision to use 497lbs of traditional Portuguese cork harvested from 225 trees in the Alentejo District as a heat shield to insulate the external fuel tanks of the Columbia space shuttle. Significantly, it was not this material which ignited in the fatal flight of 2003.

Dictatorship to democracy

After leading his country as Prime Minister for thirty-six years, at the age of 79, Salazar suddenly suffered a stroke after a fall in his home in August 1968. The state President, Américo Tomás, appointed Salazar's deputy, Caetano, as Prime Minister on 27 September 1968. For whatever reason, the incapacitated Salazar was not told of his removal from power and it is rumoured that when he died in July 1970, he still believed he was Prime Minister.

Compared with the duration of Salazar's rule, Caetano's premiership was short-lived. Calling the Estado Novo a 'social state', some progress was made during his time at the helm: he reduced press censorship, allowed the first independent elections for four decades, renamed the secret police as the *Direção Geral de Segurança* (General Directorate of Security) and softened the edges of his predecessor's regime. However, the world was changing fast – too fast for these limited changes. The Colonial Wars in Africa were taking their toll, the Cold War was still prevalent as a struggle between the superpowers, and a world in which Man had just landed on the moon (20 July 1969) was a very different era from the one faced by Salazar when he first came to power. The Estado Novo as a political concept was no longer appropriate – if it ever had been.

In 1974 came a military coup d'état (known as the Carnation Revolution) which overthrew the last vestiges of Salazar's rule. It is so-called because no shots were fired and a relieved population placed carnations down the muzzles of the militia. The 25th of April remains a national day of celebration in Portugal and the anniversary is ever-present in the form of the huge *25 de Abril* suspension bridge which crosses the River Tagus, soaring above Lisbon's port area. Red in colour, it is reminiscent of San Francisco's Golden Gate Bridge.

Construction of the bridge began in November 1962 and it was inaugurated in August 1966 as the Salazar Bridge, being renamed soon after the uprising. A towering symbol of those unhappy times, locals removed the big brass "Salazar" sign from one of the main pillars of the bridge and painted "25 de Abril" in its place. The adjacent Cristo Rei (Christ the King) statue which looks down imposingly over the river, the bridge, and Belém's imperial history, is reminiscent of the larger, mountain-top Christ the Redeemer Statue in Rio de Janeiro. Cristo Rei was opened in 1959, celebrating divine wisdom in sparing Portugal from the Second World War. Wonderful architecture it may be, but it ignores the huge income derived from the country's studied neutrality.

Figure 32. Lisbon's 25 Abril Bridge and the statue of Christ the Redeemer.

For many years after the dictatorship's end, Portugal remained a poor country. It was considered by some other Europeans to be a bit of a bad joke – impoverished, home to the highest proportion of illiterate and innumerate citizens in Western Europe, providing low quality healthcare and hampered by an infrastructure way behind other countries on the continent. Strikes by frustrated workers were common, corruption remained rife and inflation was rampant. A confused populace was uncertain how to deal with its history[6] – many wanted to forget the authoritarian times; simultaneously, architectural treasures from the glory days were decaying.

Change was needed urgently. A fundamental review of the education system, including introducing free school breakfasts, eradicated malnutrition and drove up standards and aspirations; a new curriculum provided skills for the newly-emerging economy which diversified from the traditional agriculture and long-established craft industries.

Mass tourism

Whilst Portugal had made its name for adventurous travel in the golden Age of Discoveries, trailblazing mercantile routes and bringing the exotic world of spices to Europe, travel *to* Portugal on a large scale is a relatively recent phenomenon. In Chapter 4, we saw the unintended boom in travel in the years leading up to and during the Second World War – travel undertaken either by royalty or aristocracy seeking to maintain their position of luxury and leisure away from the republican spirit of their homeland, or by refugees desperate to escape the engulfing menace of Nazism. Neither category constituted ordinary travellers looking for sunshine and leisure in a fortnight's break from work.

This latter transition was a phenomenon starting in the late 1960s, when the package holiday was born. Post-war austerity in many parts of continental Europe had given way to a rise in disposable income, if not affluence, and this coincided with the advent of jet aircraft able to reduce flight times. Large parts of the Mediterranean, from southern Spain eastwards around the northern coastline as far as Greece became transformed into holiday destinations, the accommodation being provided by cheaply and rapidly constructed concrete hotels. Kiss-me-quick hats were no longer just the province of Blackpool, Cleethorpes

---

[6] Such angst is not unusual. Berliners had a lengthy debate about restoring their war-ravaged architecture and whether it should be replaced by something entirely new and futuristic to avoid reminders of shameful times; in the UK, the cities of Bristol and Liverpool wrestled with how to deal with their wealth, so often derived through profits from slavery.

and other popular British resorts with their undependable weather. The resorts of Torremolinos, Benidorm and Magalluf beckoned – and for more adventurous travellers – willing to pay the higher airfare for a longer flight – the Greek islands, Tenerife and the Algarve were more exclusive options.

With the construction of Faro airport in the centre of the Algarve coast in 1965 began Portugal's widespread holiday trade – across the length of the Algarve with its crumbling, golden cliffs and fine sand. New resorts were established, sometimes embracing the traditional, quaint fishing villages of Vilamoura, Albufeira and Alvor; sometimes creating a newer, brasher, atmosphere dedicated to hedonistic pleasures. With the growth of tourism came regular employment – jobs in construction, hotels, bars, cafes, as well as air and road infrastructure. It became an apparently win-win situation – happy holidaymakers willing to return for inexpensive breaks in the sun and a steady income to the region in what were principally low or semi-skilled jobs. The fact that the Portuguese people were warm, welcoming hosts who, increasingly, spoke English was an added bonus.

Elsewhere in Portugal, the package holiday also caught on. Already established as a sophisticated resort area for fleeing aristocracy, the Lisbon Riviera expanded into package tourism, assisted by easy access to nearby Lisbon Portela airport, built in 1942. Expansion of the holiday trade in the 1970s meant the destruction of many of the Riviera's old buildings with their faded grandeur, replaced by the erection of new blocks for the mass market. For example, the sea front Hotel Estoril Sol became a byword for stereotypical package holiday hotels until its own demolition in 2007 and replacement by an upmarket residence. Fortunately, the imposing grandeur of the Hotel Palácio (see Chapters 4 and 5) remains.

Chapter 10

Figure 33. Modern apartments in Parque das Nações, Lisbon.

As with any business, suppliers evolve to meet changing customer expectations. Today, golf is a significant tourist business across many parts of Portugal, offering manicured courses with spectacular views. If you explore the pedestrianised shopping areas of Cascais, for example, you will encounter many restaurants advertising two atypical Portuguese specialities – curry and pizza. These offerings have been devised specifically for the golfing market. In the last decade many discerning, independent travellers have sought the individuality of staying in Pousadas, a network of historic accommodation (like Spain's Paradors) located in some of Portugal's most interesting and beautiful locations. Originally created as rest houses in areas that did not offer other accommodation, today castles, palaces, monasteries and manor houses have all become examples of pousadas.

Football

During Salazar's time, it was often said that the Portuguese masses were kept in their place by a diet of fado, Fatima and football. Today Portugal boasts many internationally fêted players, as well as clubs.

Travelling west from Lisbon airport you will pass both the Sporting Clube de Portugal (commonly known in the UK as Sporting Lisbon) and the Benfica stadia within two kilometres of each other, straddling either side of the Avenida Eusébio da Silva Ferreira, named after arguably the country's most famous player, Eusébio. Followed with a passion, football has a number of newspapers entirely dedicated to it and the prestige and influence of its main teams, with Porto making up the "Três Grandes" (or big Three). In popular culture terms, these famous teams offer well-known, international ambassadors who have done much to raise the profile of Portugal among sports fans globally. Links with Brazilian teams, players and competitions (for example, Brazil as host nation of the 2014 World Cup) are prized. One of the game's most famous and celebrated players, Cristiano Ronaldo, is Portuguese and is revered in his home town of Funchal, the capital of the island of Madeira, where his dedication to improving the lives of young people is regarded highly, the more so for its muted stance.

The future

Portugal has found its way into the 21st century, developing tourism but still heavily dependent upon EU funding for infrastructure development and employment in new scientific, research, and industrial sectors. It has become a significant player in the so-called European Research Area. The country's Prime Minister from 2002-2004, Manuel Barroso (himself a former law professor), became the 11th President of the European Commission from 2004-2014 and, whilst he held an impartial pan-Europe view, this decade also saw the transformation of Portugal into a full European state. Notwithstanding its EU financial bailout, the country has avoided some of the extreme economic calamities in neighbouring Spain, and still cherishes the Anglo-Portuguese Alliance. Its links with Brazil and that country's dynamic economy and development remain crucial economically and culturally.

Many younger Portuguese are genuinely oblivious of their nation's wartime activities but the impact of the wolfram trade is still felt. You can undertake a walking tour in Lisbon entitled 'City of Spies', the Palácio Hotel openly shares its past history as a centre for spies and whilst the Atlântico Hotel has been demolished, the sales brochure for the replacement upmarket apartments on its former site refer openly to its wartime past. Moreover, in the mining areas, the remnants of the

Chapter 10

fossicking mines are visible[7] and the former dwellings in Panasqueira are advertised, for the imaginative, as suitable for renovation into holiday cottages.

The nation has moved forward to become a key European player, enjoying high esteem amongst holidaymakers, football fans, scientists and industrialists alike. Many visitors are unaware of its history of war-time intrigue and, whilst the country continues to develop in so many ways in the sunlight of democracy, the full history of its darker, dictatorial past from a different era will remain, like the shadowy figures in Rossio Square, enveloped in a certain secrecy.

---

[7] See *Emma's House in Portugal* for a variety of images.
http://www.emmashouseinportugal.com/living-in-portugal/volframio-portugal-in-ww2/

Glossary

Abwehr | Meaning 'defence' in the German language, the Abwehr was the German Secret Service. See index for more detail of where Abwehr is referred to.

Battle of the Bulge | Taking place in December 1944 in the Ardennes region of Belgium, this battle was one of the final set-piece battles on the Western Front. Having made quicker progress across France from the Normandy D-Day beaches than was anticipated, the Allies were met with fierce resistance by this German offensive. It was well-known for its harsh conditions and for the fervour with which it was fought. Allied victory meant rapid progress to Berlin.

CADC | The Academic Christian Democracy Centre was founded in 1901 at the University of Coimbra (Portugal's most prestigious university where Salazar studied and taught). It was, and remains, dedicated to a Roman Catholic perspective on the nature of democracy and acts as a think tank for debating such issues, particularly relating to anti-clerical stances by government.

Carnation Revolution | A military coup in Lisbon on 25 April, 1974, by which the Estado Novo regime (see below) was overthrown. It was so-called because of its peaceful nature and the way in which Lisboans placed carnation stems in the muzzles of the soldiers' rifles. The date is not only commemorated annually as marking Portugal's return to democracy but also in the name of the suspension bridge crossing the River Tagus in Lisbon.

Double-Cross System | Known also as the XX System, this counter-espionage operation by MI5 (see below) achieved significant success. Agents of the Abwehr (see above) were recruited in order to spy on Nazi operations and report these to the Twenty Committee of MI5. In particular Operation Fortitude and Operation Overlord (respectively the secret operations relating to the location of the D-Day landings and the execution of D-Day itself) were success stories of the Double Cross System. Two of their agents' stories are explained in Chapter 5.

ENIGMA code | Now the subject of several major films, the British efforts to successfully break the code of the German ENIGMA encryption machines was a major wartime achievement. Success meant that the Axis powers were not able to communicate to each other. An army of mathematicians, linguists and other code breakers was employed at the British Government's Code and Cypher School at Bletchley Park, which is now home to the National Museum of Computing. Alan Turing is the most famous of the code breakers but it was a joint effort by many skilled specialists, sworn to secrecy.

Estado Novo | Meaning 'New State' in Portuguese, this was the name by which the authoritarian Second Republic of 1933 was known. Its founding leader right through to 1968 was Dr António de Oliveira Salazar (see Chapter 3).

FBI | The Federal Bureau of Investigation is the domestic security organisation of the United States. Its activities are similar to those of the British MI5 (see below). Its most famous head was J Edgar Hoover.

MI5 | Military Intelligence 5 (hence MI5) is the British government security service. According to its website, its role is "to protect the UK, its citizens and interests at home and overseas against threats to national security". Politically, it is answerable to the British Home Secretary. During the Second World War, some of its responsibilities included the Double-Cross team and monitoring the Abwehr.

MI6 | Military Intelligence 6 (hence MI6) is the British secret intelligence service. According to its website, its role is "gathering intelligence outside the UK in support of the government's security, defence, foreign and economic policies". Politically, it is answerable to the British Foreign Secretary. During the Second World War, some of its responsibilities included Bletchley Park's code breaking operations. One of its key Iberian agents was Kim Philby, who later defected to Russia.

Pearl Harbor | Located on the Hawaiian island of Oahu, west of Honolulu, Pearl Harbor became infamous as the site of the Japanese attack on the US Pacific naval fleet on 7 December 1941. This surprise airstrike immediately brought the US into the Second World War, as it destroyed 188 US aircraft, killed 2,403 Americans and wounded over 1,000 others.

Spanish Civil War | Lasting from 1936-1939, the Spanish Civil War divided the nation between Republicans and Nationalists (led by

General Franco). As victor, Franco led the nation from 1939 until his death in 1975. A non-combatant nation in the Second World War, Spain nevertheless enjoyed support from the Nazis during the Civil War and became sympathetic to their cause thereafter. As the only land neighbour to Portugal, an uneasy alliance developed between the two countries, both fearing the spread of Communism, but with Salazar distrustful of Franco's own policies.

Third Reich | 'Reich' means 'empire' in German. The Third Reich refers to the Nazi government of Adolf Hitler from 1933-1945. Hitler believed that he was creating a third German empire – a successor to the Holy Roman Empire and the German empire formed by Chancellor Bismarck in the nineteenth century.

U-boat | 'Untersee-boot' or 'under sea boat'. During the Second World War, U-boats were a major threat, particularly to the Atlantic convoys of merchant vessels which kept the UK supplied with many foodstuffs and raw materials. Unlike modern nuclear submarines, U-boats were more ship-like in appearance as they spent much of their time on the surface, diving only when necessary. With a major base in St Nazaire in occupied France, the Bay of Biscay was known as 'The Valley of Death' to U-boat crews because of RAF supremacy in hunting them down. This reduced attacks on British vessels on the Portugal run, as a total of 66 U-boats were sunk by the RAF in the Bay alone, a significant proportion of total losses.

Bibliography

Bacher L. (1996). *Max Ophuls in the Hollywood Studios*. New Jersey: Rutgers University Press.

Ball G W. (1968). *The Discipline of Power*. Boston, Mass.: Little, Brown.

Birmingham D. (2003). *A Concise History of Portugal*. 2nd ed. Cambridge: Cambridge University Press.

Bower T. (1997). *Nazi Gold*. London: HarperCollins.

Brandao F N. Epidemiology of Venereal Disease in Portugal during the Second World War. *British Journal of Venereal Diseases*, 36, no. 2 (1960).

Brown J et al. (2014). *The Rough Guide to Portugal*. London: Rough Guides.

Cabel C. (2008). *Ian Fleming's Secret War*. Barnsley: Pen & Sword.

Christopher J. (2014). *Sherman M4 Medium Tank*. Stroud: Amberley Publishing.

Corse E. (2014). *A Battle for Neutral Europe: British Cultural Propaganda During the Second World War*. London: Bloomsbury.

D'Assac P D'A. (1967). *Salazar*. Paris: La Table Ronde.

Day P. (2014). *The Bedbug: Klop Ustinov – Britain's Most Ingenious Spy*. London: Biteback Publishing.

Dougherty M J. (2010). *Tanks Compared & Contrasted: From World War I To The Present Day*. London: Amber Books.

Drucker P F. (2003). *The Essential Drucker*. New York: Harper Business Books.

Eccles, D. (1983). *By Safe Hand: Letters of Sybil and David Eccles, 1939-1942*. Bodley Head: London.

Egerton F C C. (1943). *Salazar: Rebuilder of Portugal*. London: Hodder & Stoughton.

Farndon J & Parker S. (2012). *The Complete Illustrated Guide to Minerals, Rocks & Fossils of the World*. Wigston, Leics.: Southwater.

Ferro A. (1939). *Salazar, Portugal and her Leader*. London: Faber & Faber.

Fleming I. (1953) *Casino Royale*. London: Jonathan Cape.

Fortey G. (2012). *World War I & II Tanks*. Wigston, Leics.: Southwater.

Fortey G & Livesey J. (2012). *The Complete Guide to Tanks and Armoured Fighting Vehicles*. Wigston, Leics.: Southwater.

Gallagher T. (1982). *Portugal: A Twentieth Century Interpretation*. Manchester: Manchester University Press

Gander T J. (2006). *Panzer Kampfwagen I & II*. Hersham, Surrey: Ian Allan Publishing.

Gentry C. (1991). *J Edgar Hoover: The Man and the Secrets*. Norton: New York.

Georgel J. (1981). *Le Salazarisme: Historie et Bilan*. 1926-1974. Paris: Cujas.

Independent Commission of Experts Switzerland – Second World War: Switzerland and Refugees in the Nazi Era. (1999). Bern.

Jeffrey K. (2010). *MI6: The History of the Secret Intelligence Service 1909-1949*. London: Bloomsbury.

Kaplan M. (2013). *Lisbon is Sold Out! The Daily lives of Jewish Refugees in Portugal During World War II*. New York: Tikvah Center for Law and Jewish civilization.

Kay H. (1970). *Salazar and Modern Portugal*. New York: Hawthorn Publishers.

Knapp B. (1975). *Maurice Maeterlinck*. Boston, Mass.: Thackery Publishers.

Lage M O. (2011). The Significance Of The Tua Valley In The Context Of The Portuguese Wolfram Boom (1st Half of The XX Century). In McCants, A (ed) et al. Railroads in Historical Context: construction, costs and consequences. FOTZUA; Vila Nova de Gaia:

MIT (Portugal), EDP, University of Minho, 2011. Vol 1, p15-43. (Proceedings of the 1st International Conference of the International and Transdisciplinary Project FozTua, 2011).

Lloyd-Jones S. (2000). *A Short History of the First Republic*. Instituto Universitário de Lisboa. Lisboa. Working paper.

Lochery N. (2011). *Lisbon: War in the Shadows of the City of Light, 1939-1945*. New York: Public Affairs.

Louca A. *Nazigold für Portugal: Hitler und Salazar*. Wien: Holzhausen. 2002. 281.

Milton G. (2011). *Wolfram: The Boy Who Went to War*. London: Sceptre.

Page M. (2002). *The First Global Village: How Portugal Changed the World*. (19th ed.; 2014). Alfragide: Casa das Letras.

Peters T & Waterman R Jr. (1982). *In Search of Excellence: Lessons from America's Best-Run Companies*. New York: HarperCollins.

Popov D. Spy / Counter-Spy: The Autobiography of Dusko Popov. (1975). Greenwich, Conn.: Fawcett.

Preston P. (1994). *Franco: A Biography*. London: Basic Books.

Sayers D. (2013). *Azores*. 5th ed. Bradt: Buckinghamshire.

Seligo I. (1942). *A day at Alcobaca* in *Delfina – short stories from a German journalist's life in wartime Lisbon*. Frankfurt: Societäts-verlag.

Sergueiev L. (1968). *Secret Service Rendered: An Agent in the Espionage Duel Preceding the Invasion of France*. London: William Kimber.

Symington M et al. (2014). *Portugal.* London: Dorling Kindersley.

Teixera M. (2008). Caught on the Periphery: *Portuguese Neutrality during World War II and Anglo-American Negotiations with Salazar*. University of Pennsylvania. Thesis submitted and available at: http://repository.upenn.edu/hist_honors/14/

Walker D E. (1957). *Lunch With A Stranger*. London: Allan Wingate.

Weber R. (2011). *The Lisbon Route: Entry and Escape in Nazi Europe*. Plymouth, UK: Ivan R Dee.

Wheeler D L. (1986). The Price of Neutrality: Portugal, the Wolfram Question and World War II. *Luso-Brazilian Review*, Vol 23. No 1.

Wilsford D (ed.). (1995). *Political Leaders of contemporary Western Europe: A Biographical Dictionary*. Westport, Connecticut: Greenwood Press.

Wilson J. Tungsten miner hardens big plans in Devon. *Financial Times*, 27 January, 2014.

Wilson R. (1999). *A Small Death in Lisbon*. London: HarperCollins.

Online references
and resources

In addition to extracts of the above books available online, there are a number of other interesting and freely-accessible resources, including those referred to in footnotes. Additional resources include:

A package of free resources in Portuguese on YouTube® relating to a number of the ruined mines and aspects relating to the life of mining communities:

https://www.youtube.com/watch?v=EYmy-RQjoqw

A number of these resources have been assembled and edited by Professor Otilia Lage, who acted as scientific consultant and member of the board of the following project (in English) www.routesofwolfram.eu

The excellent blog by Emma Brunton on aspects of living in Portugal can be found at: www.emmashouseinportugal.com . This includes several blogs on spying and wolfram.

An interesting and illuminating lunch-time lecture on the plight of Jewish refugees in wartime Lisbon by Professor Neill Lochery of University College London. Available at: https://www.youtube.com/watch?v=Kr9sdiZOCQc#t=48

Index

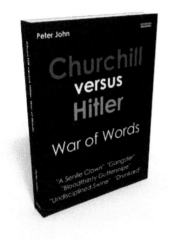

Churchill versus Hitler: War of Words by Peter John

"A senile clown", "Bloodthirsty Guttersnipe", "Undisciplined Swine", "Gangster", "Drunkard"

Adolf Hitler and Winston Churchill clashed for years in public as their opinions of each other and feuding helped determine the course of the Second World War. As diplomatic and military episodes unfolded - both men analysed, commented upon, and taunted each other with Churchill continuing to do so for many years after Hitler's death. Yet, until now, there has been no dedicated, detailed history of the men's rivalry.

Based on three years of research in archives across Britain, Germany and the United States, Churchill versus Hitler: War of Words chronicles the Second World War, and much more, through the protagonists' speeches, writings and private conversations, and includes revealing perspectives from other major figures including Goebbels, Roosevelt and Chamberlain. This fascinating book sets the battle for victory in the context of the momentous historical developments of the age and new light is shed upon various incidents in both men's lives including their first encounters of each other, and their abortive meeting in 1932. What becomes clear is that the opinions of the two leaders were more complicated and changeable than is often assumed.

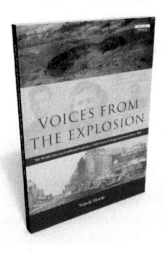

Voices from the Explosion: RAF Fauld, the World's Largest Accidental Blast, 1944
by Valerie Hardy

The story, told for the first time from eyewitness accounts, of the world's largest manmade pre-nuclear explosion. It happened at R.A.F. Fauld bomb store on 27th November 1944 and killed 70 people. The author's family farm was damaged in the blast but the family survived. Neighbouring friends, and their farm, disappeared forever.

Today, a massive crater survives as a lasting reminder of the nearly 4,000 tons of bombs and shells that blew up, registering on seismographs as far away as Casablanca. Six million gallons of reservoir water turned 90 feet of solid earth falling from the sky into mud, which engulfed a plaster works and its workers.

In this fascinating and expertly researched book, author Valerie Hardy crafts a compelling and unforgettable read. Bringing eyewitness stories together, the tragedy is relived and provides an extraordinary insight into the disaster that unfolded that winter morning.

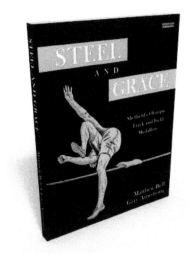

Steel and Grace: Sheffield's Olympic Track and Field Medallists by Matthew Bell and Gary Armstrong

There is a British city that has produced some of the most exceptional individuals to ever grace the Olympic Games. A city that has developed many of the finest athletes to wear our national colours. Offering a unique insight, and drawing on extensive archives, Steel and Grace: Sheffield's Olympic Track and Field Medallists examines the athletes of 'Steel City' and their contributions to the Olympic Games over more than a century.

The book examines the lives and careers of athletes who stood on the medal podium and positions their achievements within the political events that impacted upon the Games: in Berlin as Hitler showcased his Nazi regime; in Munich when terrorists murdered 11 Israeli athletes; in Moscow when British athletes competed against the wishes of the UK Government at the height of the Cold War.

Steel and Grace details the accomplishments and biographies of both well-known and sadly forgotten Sheffield athletes. These include the first man in history to run the 1,500 metres in under four minutes and the athlete who completed the last eight miles of an Olympic marathon with blistered and bloodied feet to win a silver medal. The same man survived the Olympic race that nearly killed several of its competitors.

Steel and Grace is an exceptional contribution to Olympic literature; its exploration into the track and field history of Sheffield has no parallel. Bringing to life tales of gracious sportsmanship, fierce rivalry, heartbreak and joy, it highlights the value of Sheffield's contributions and questions where the origins of the dedication required to achieve Olympic success might lie.

Printed in the USA
CPSIA information can be obtained
at www.ICGtesting.com
LVHW021036171123
764154LV00011B/241

9 781911 121077